BE HGV AWARE

CYCLISTS

Information and Advice to help You Stay Safe

Richard Bailey

Cover designed by Richard Bailey

Printed in the United Kingdom

First Printing: Feb 2019
RDAB Assured Ltd

ISBN-9781726685344

This book is dedicated to the memory of those that have lost their lives through incidents on our roads.

This book is also dedicated to the one person that has always been there for me, my Mum.
Without her support I do not know what I would have done.
Thank you.

I would also like to thank Claire, Louise and David for their assistance with my terrible grammar! If there are still mistakes then it is only because I overlooked their suggestions.

Disclaimer

The information enclosed within this book is given out as advice only. It is a general overview of HGV visual limitations and how those limitations may affect you while using the public highways. By choosing to read this book you accept that the Author, Richard Bailey and/or RDAB Assured Limited, cannot be held responsible for your decisions. If using the enclosed information while on the road all decisions remain yours.

This book has been written with Right-hand drive vehicles in mind, with examples from the Authors experiences and while driving on roads in the United Kingdom. The information enclosed may well be relevant in other countries (in an opposite capacity) but please be careful not to confuse specific details if you are in a Left-hand Drive country.

A Qualification (something else to read!)

Before you start this book I would like to address something. When I first had the idea of Be HGV Aware I was well aware that I did not know all of the issues and concerns of Cyclists with regard to HGVs. I needed help. As a result I made contact with a number of the UKs leading cycling and road safety organisations. I wanted to know what their thoughts were on my idea and whether they would be willing to offer any advice or feedback on what I planned to do. Unfortunately only *Brake*, the Road Safety Charity, offered any help. While I did receive limited replies these were only to say that others would not be willing to help me. The reason I mention this is not to shame those cycling organisations for not helping me; I mention this because I want you to know that I do not pretend to know what all of your concerns are. In this book I have tried to offer my best advice and information on a very sensitive subject, but I understand that there may well be concerns not covered within. If it does not then I can only apologise. As I say this is not a criticism of those organisations. It is just to say this book may not cover everything, but I hope it covers enough to help in your safety.

Image Key

Throughout the book I have created images to help explain the text. Here is a quick guide to the imagery that I have used.

Red/shaded area

This will indicate what CANNOT BE SEEN when the Driver is looking in certain directions.

White area

This will indicate what CAN BE SEEN when the Driver is looking in certain directions.

Cyclist: Birds-eye view

This represents a Cyclist from above in the birds-eye images.

Cyclist: Three dimensional view

This represents a Cyclist in the 3D images.

Rigid HGV: Three dimensional view

A Rigid-bodied HGV is a very large, very wide, very long vehicle that has a Cab and large cargo area (any discussion regarding Articulated HGVs will be high-lighted).

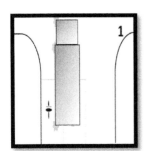

Rigid HGV: Birds-eye view

This represents a HGV in the birds-eye view images.

Yellow/light grey 'HGV Driver Glances'

The yellow/light grey lines will show where the HGV Driver is looking i.e.in a certain mirror or a particular direction.

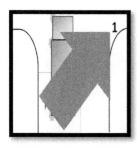

Image in discussion

The image being discussed within the text will be marked by a number in the top corner, like this number **1.**

Introduction

Thank you for opening this little book. I really appreciate you doing so. I know that it's because you want to help keep yourself safer so I thank you for taking the time to look at, what I know, will help keep you safer while cycling on our roads.

As we are at the beginning I want to make something very clear. I am not going to pretend this book is the silver bullet that will stop incidents between Cyclists and HGV Drivers. What I do hope is by reading this book it might stop *you* making a decision that puts you at an increased chance of danger. By that I don't mean that Cyclists are to blame for incidents; what I mean is that if you are in a position where it is your decision I hope that by reading this book that decision can be more informed. As a HGV Driver of over 20 years I know that I see so many Cyclists *unknowingly* putting themselves into potential danger because they don't know what the HGV Driver is dealing with inside the HGV. Ultimately, that is my motivation: to help you stay safer on the road by informing you of what the HGV Driver is dealing with. I say 'safer' as no matter how much you think you know or how good you think you are, there is always something you can learn. Knowledge is never a bad thing to have and I may just get you thinking about something you have never thought of before.

My name is Richard and I am the creator of 'Be HGV Aware'. I wanted to try and do something after seeing a Cyclist killed in a collision with a HGV. I do not want what happened to that Cyclist, and their family, to happen to you. I am a HGV Driver; I am also a Cyclist so I thought I would be able to offer a more balanced approach to the sensitive subject of cycling safety and HGVs. I know this book will receive criticism from those who say that it is 'victim-blaming'. At this point I want to say that this book is not about victim-blaming. I know some people will project their biases on to this book but it is purely about giving people information that they may not have. I know that not all HGV Drivers are angels. I know some have been responsible for the deaths of other road-users, and I know that in some cases it was down to their complete lack of professionalism. It fills me with anger, and hurt, when I hear about the deaths of Cyclists or Pedestrians just because of some selfish, unprofessional HGV Driver kills or maims as a result of their dangerous behaviour. So as you read this book I want you to remember that am not making excuses for HGV Drivers but I know, having been one, that there are HGV Drivers doing everything they can to make sure they are not involved in a collision on the road despite the design of the vehicles they drive, out-of-date road infrastructure and the behaviour of others, yet may still become involved in a collision because they happen to be looking in one direction when a Cyclist was positioned in another.

For every incident that takes place there are those that will say the HGV Driver was at fault, similarly there are those who will say the Cyclist was at fault. Each incident needs to be looked at individually and the facts need to be ascertained before any blame is apportioned. If the HGV Driver was found to be doing everything possible to see their surroundings, can you blame someone who cannot see their surroundings fully due to the design of the HGV, the road layout or the activity around them? Moreover, can you blame a Cyclist for *unknowingly* putting themselves into a position that they didn't realise *was* dangerous or put into a position because of poor infrastructure? It may be uncomfortable for some to admit but unfortunately the answer to both is no, you cannot always blame the other but, if a mistake is made by either, someone should not be paying for it with their life.

So this book is not about blame because, ultimately, does it really matter who to blame when someone is dead in the most horrific of ways possible? As the Cyclist you may have been in the right. You or your family may gain some sort of financial pay-out. There may be feelings of relief and vindication at someone being prosecuted. There may even be a custodial sentence but that will never replace a loved one. You or your loved one may be dead and nothing will ever change that. I don't want that to happen.

So, as I said, this book is not about blame. It is about giving information and advice about the visual limitations surrounding HGVs to those that may not have it.

The frustrating thing is that while HGV Drivers know what the limitations are, this information would be much more useful in the hands of those that interact with HGVs and large vehicles on a daily basis. Things are changing: HGV design, road design and HGV Driver awareness and training. One day I genuinely hope that this book won't matter because there will be cycling infrastructure across the whole of our road network. This will mean more people taking up cycling and as those numbers increase driving culture within the UK will start to accept Cyclists as equal road-users, but because none of those ideals are fully there yet this book, at the moment, does matter.

There are lots of people on the roads who do not understand how or why a HGV moves the way it does…and in fairness why would they? Do you? (I would say you probably don't as you're reading this book…and thanks!), Unfortunately though not having this information means that some increase their chances of becoming involved in a collision with a HGV and *that* is the key: not having this information *increases* your chances of becoming involved in an incident.

While we use the road we are relying on others to keep us safe. We want all road users to think about others and how decisions they take may negatively affect us. That may not always be the case but we do rely heavily on others for our safety. Whether you know it or are happy to admit it means you are relying on HGV Drivers for your safety. I want you to read this book to *decrease* the chance of you becoming involved in an incident…and while it may be controversial to say, I want you to *not* rely on HGV Drivers for your safety. I want *you* to rely on you for your safety. The reason I say this is because of what I am going to show you in this book.

I do not want to scare you off the road. I will not tell you what to do but what I do want to get across is that sometimes, due to the fluid nature of the road, the design of HGVs (which is a debate in its self); the size of the Blind-spots; the instant, ever-changing nature of the Blind-spots; the need to look in certain directions at certain times; a particular road layout; the level of activity at a certain junction or due to your size or speed, you may not have been seen...and that is when a HGV Driver *is* doing everything they can to look for you as well as actually drive the HGV, so imagine what cannot be seen by some of those HGV Drivers who *are not* doing everything they can to look for you.

Now I do have to say that most of the last twelve years of my HGV driving career has been based in London. As a result this book is based on my experiences within an urban environment and a high population, commuting city...and the aggressive, impatient behaviour that seems to come with that environment. I know that not all urban areas have seen the massive increase of cycling that there has been in London; not all urban areas have the same challenging, outdated road systems or the high levels of congestion. The intensity and 'attention-absorbing' nature of London driving may not be the same everywhere, but if I can get across to you how difficult it can be to drive a HGV at its most intense then you can take bits of this book to help you wherever you cycle.

As I have mentioned, I want to help keep Cyclists safer on the roads. That is my motivation because of what I saw. I know that this book is only going to play a very small part in road safety but ultimately, I want to help others. As you read this book I would really like you to remember that. Depending on your view-point you may get angry at what I suggest. You may not agree with everything written within these pages and for the record, and I will state it again, I know this book will not be the silver bullet that stops collisions between HGV and Bicycle, but in its simplest form this book is about giving you information and advice that you may never have thought of. You can choose what to do with this information, but I know it will add to your road safety knowledge. I hope that you find it interesting as well.

Richard

What does this book contain?

To help you understand HGV Drivers' visual limitations I will start with the basics of what a HGV Driver sees. The obvious place to begin is with the HGV mirrors. Once you know how many mirrors there are, what each mirror shows...and doesn't show, you will start to get an idea that the HGV Driver cannot see everywhere at all times. I will then discuss the Blind-spots (areas the HGV Driver cannot see) surrounding the HGV. I will introduce you to the two types of Blind-spot that I have defined: the HGV Driver's 'Observational Limitations' and then 'Physical Obstructions' caused by the Mirrors, the vehicle design and the Trailer.

Once you have this knowledge I will then discuss various situations you may find yourself in such as junctions, traffic lights, roundabouts, encountering a turning HGV, and the creation of the 'Illusion of Space' which is very important for your safety.

I will also discuss things that I want you to think about while cycling on the road....things that I think about when I ride my bicycle.

Throughout the book I really want to get across that being on the road is not full of textbook situations. It is a fluid, real environment. This 'fluidity' may mean you suddenly find yourself in a position that you had not seen developing. This is also true for HGV Drivers but this can be the frustrating reality of being on the road.

Consequently, throughout the book I may not be able to cover every detail, every eventuality but I know that what I am going to show you will give you a very good knowledge about HGVs when on the road.

Don't Let the Height Fool You

Before I take you on an *exciting* and *wonderful* world of the HGV (!) I want to dispel one myth that I think a lot of people believe. There is a misconception by those who have never been inside a HGV that just because the HGV Driver sits so high in the Cab they have an amazing view of their surroundings, and can see everything around them. This is not true. Don't get me wrong, when I am looking forward I am able to read the road a lot better than a car driver. My forward view is rarely obscured and I am able to see hundreds of meters in front of me, if the conditions and environment allow me, but this book will show you that because there are so many areas a HGV Driver must look, that means certain areas may not have been seen when you happen to be in them…often because those areas aren't the most at risk of hitting something. The height helps HGV Drivers but it also hinders them too. Equally, over the last few years some HGV Cabs have become stupidly high. This has occurred due to the need of cleaner engines and lower emissions. Engines have required more filters and larger exhaust systems to make sure the fumes expelled by the engine are cleaner for the environment, which is great! Unfortunately the width and length of HGVs cannot be increased as this would break vehicle safety size regulations so the only easy space manufacturers have is to build upwards. This height has led to the size of some Blind-spots increasing, and the chance of you being seen is now even lower for some HGV Drivers.

One other factor to consider is that the HGV Driver will spend the majority of their time concentrating on manoeuvring the HGV in a forward direction. HGV Drivers will regularly look into their mirrors but you must remember that the biggest potential danger of collision for a HGV Driver, for any road user, will always remain at the front of the HGV so this is where the HGV Driver will be looking for the majority of the time. Yes HGV Drivers are taught to look into their mirrors as often as they can and to look in certain mirrors for certain manoeuvres so that may sound strange...you probably know that HGVs have mirrors so the Driver can see the sides of their vehicle...but the biggest chance of collision for a HGV Driver, for any road user, is going to be from the front so that is where the HGV Driver will concentrate a lot of their attention. This is when you may be missed.

I will expand on this throughout the book but let me introduce to you the Mirrors that are found on modern HGVs.

Mirrors

How many mirrors does a modern HGV have?

Have a guess

2? 3? 4? 5? 6? 7?

It's 6.

Well done if you guessed correctly! If you didn't then you've already learnt something and my book is working. Yay!

Modern HGVs will have 6 mirrors to help the HGV Driver look at their surroundings. Each mirror shows a different view and each one must be looked into at various times to allow the HGV Driver to see what is around their vehicle. The mirrors should be clean and positioned by the HGV Driver for their own preferences before they set off on their day's driving. This may not always be the reality but this is what is expected of a HGV Driver as part of their daily checks prior to taking that vehicle on the road. 6 mirrors do show quite a good view of the surroundings but what I would like you to look at in the following pictures is how big a portion of the mirror is actually taken up by the body of the HGV itself. Personally I like to see the side of my HGV in my mirrors as I like to see how close other objects are to me. Other Drivers may position the mirrors slightly differently. Whatever the position though, the mirrors must be correct for the HGV Driver to see what they need to see.

On the next few pages we will take a look at each mirror individually.

THE CLASS 2 'MAIN' MIRRORS

The Class 2 mirrors are the Main, larger mirrors a HGV Driver will tend to use as they offer an undistorted view of the sides of the HGV. There is one on each side and as you can see the white 'views' are quite narrow. One point to remember is that the HGV Driver cannot see both large mirrors at the same time, HGVs are just too wide to allow the HGV Driver to see into them both at the same time.

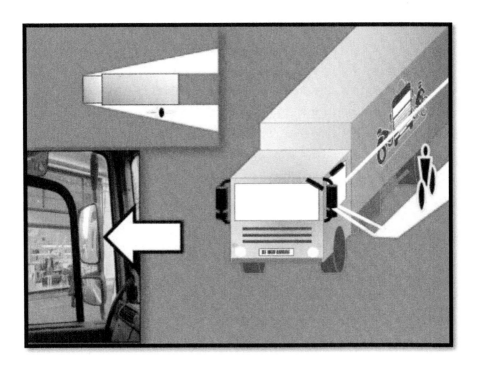

The view from this mirror does not allow the HGV Driver to see straight down. If you are positioned just forward of the white view, and the HGV Driver looks into their left, Main mirror then you may not have been seen.

CLASS 4 'WIDE-ANGLE' MIRRORS

These are the Class 4, or Wide-angle mirrors. They were introduced to help alleviate the narrowness caused by the Main

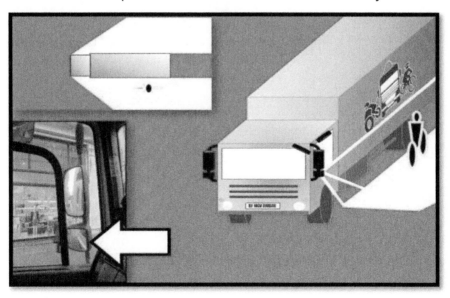

mirrors. There is one on each side and they are a convex mirror (the lens bends outwards). This means the image is slightly bowed and takes a fraction longer for the Driver to process the image. It is great for seeing a wider view surrounding the HGV Cab. The right-hand mirror offers a very good view of the side of the HGV (if it's being looked into) but unfortunately, the left-hand mirror still does not allow the Driver to see straight down.

Using the image on the right. It is a massive improvement but if you are forward of this view when the HGV Driver looks into this mirror there is a very good chance you will not be seen.

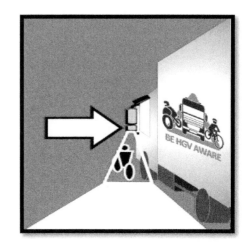

CLASS 5 'CLOSE PROXIMITY' MIRROR

This is the Class 5, or 'Close Proximity' mirror. It was introduced to try and alleviate the visual limitations caused by the left Main and Wide-angle mirrors that I have mentioned above. This is another convex mirror so takes a fraction longer to recognise detail within the mirror.

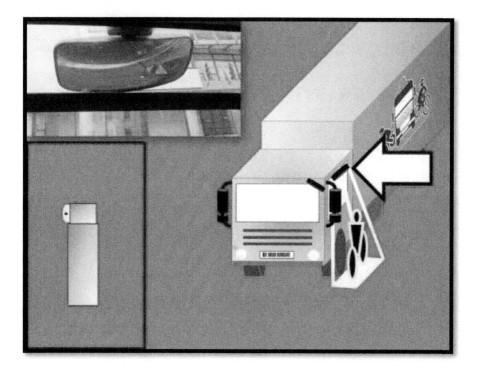

They can be useful but when the HGV Driver uses this mirror they are looking over their left shoulder. It does mean they cannot really see anything else of their surroundings.

This will mean the HGV Driver cannot look for very long and you will be very lucky if you happen to be in that mirror as the HGV Driver uses it.

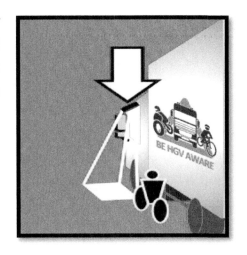

CLASS 6 'FRONT PROJECTION' MIRROR

This is the Class 6, Front projection/'front bumper' mirror. It was introduced to help the HGV Driver see the close area in front of

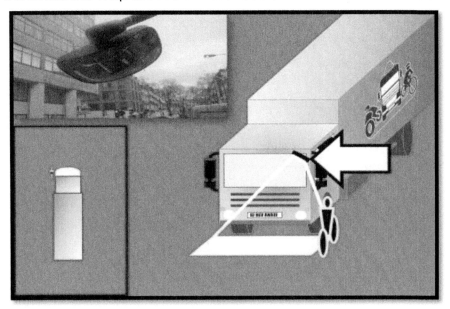

the lower part of their Cab. This is also a convex mirror. They can be positioned above the centre of the windscreen or on the left-hand side (as shown above). Again, the view is quite small but it does offer a good view of the front of the HGV.

This is especially useful when stopped at a Pedestrian crossing or junction to make sure the front area of their HGV is clear.

This does not help you too much as you will not often be that close to the HGV front. You may be lucky and just be seen in the extreme left of the mirror, if the HGV Driver is using it.

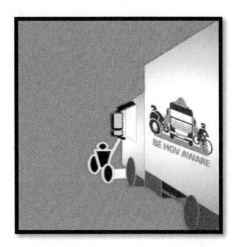

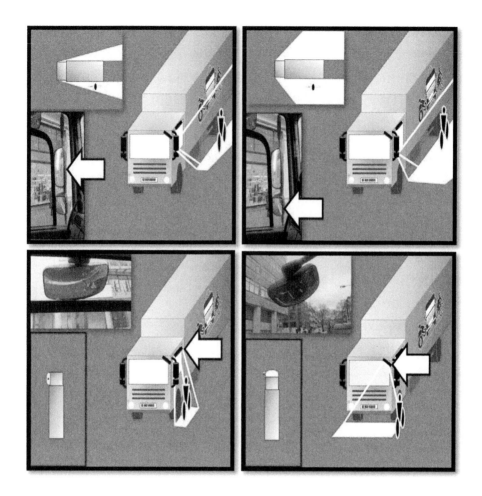

Those are the mirrors. All together they can show a pretty good view of what surrounds the HGV. What I would also like you to think about is that 6 mirrors are actually quite a lot. Of course they are needed but I cycle with one mirror that is positioned at the end of my handlebar. Cars have 3 mirrors to check left, right and behind. A HGV has 6 mirrors! Two on each side because neither shows the complete full side of a HGV plus one to see the front bumper and another to show the left side of the Cab. The average time vehicle drivers look into a mirror is 0.7 seconds. Sometimes a HGV Driver may be able to look longer into a particular mirror but imagine if they have to look into all the mirrors, for example, as they pull away from a stationary position. Cyclists may have surrounded the HGV at a set of traffic lights and it's going to take a good few seconds to check all of the mirrors. As they check, they know that what may have been clear originally could have changed so need to look again…and again! Also, as the human eye only really picks up detailed images in a small area of its vision, this may be key to whether you have been seen or not.

We have peripheral vision and this does pick up movement but remember, as a HGV Driver, all of their surroundings are moving so they are constantly having to fight their natural instinct to look at movement. Imagine trying to look into the left mirror, focus on the objects within that mirror while the outside world is rushing past that mirror. The brain and eyes want to react to the movement, and react, but at the same time the HGV Driver has to train themselves not to react to this movement as the mirror must be focused on…but what if *you* are the movement to the side of that mirror? Does that mean you have been missed while I've looked around my HGV? Maybe.

Other Variables

These conditions may not exist at all times but it is useful for you to know.

Reflections

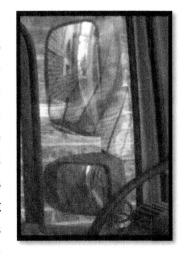

A common issue is that of reflections within the Cab. Due to the large amounts of glass used for the windscreens reflections from within and from outside the Cab can obscure the view of the mirrors at times. This doesn't happen all the time, and does tend to occur on the left-hand side, but this can't be alleviated on some HGVs by simply opening the window (as can be seen here).

Sun

The sun may not constantly be like this but when I took this photo I had been in slow moving and stationary traffic for about 5 minutes. It was a straight road and even with sunglasses I was unable to see anything in my left and right mirrors for that time. This was a lovely sunny, winter's day so the sun was bright but very low. If you do see your shadow cast in front of you when on the road then there is a chance the sun will be in the HGV Driver's mirrors.

Darkness

Obviously dark conditions make it harder to see. That is the same for everyone and in HGV mirrors the world does become very 2 dimensional. If there is a line of headlights in the mirror it is often difficult to distinguish anything else within that mirror depending on surrounding light conditions. Add in some rain and it becomes even more difficult to see. The droplets will act like individual mirrors  reflecting headlights and distorting the flat surface of the mirror.

What I must also emphasise here is that mirrors only work when the HGV Driver is looking into them. That may sound obvious but I would like you to remember that the mirrors are on the left *and* the right of the HGV.

I would like you to try a little experiment for me. Imagine you are staring straight ahead at the 12 o'clock positon on a clock face. To your left is 9 o'clock and to your right is 3 o'clock.

- Put your left arm just forward of 9 o'clock and your right arm at 1 o'clock as shown in the picture.

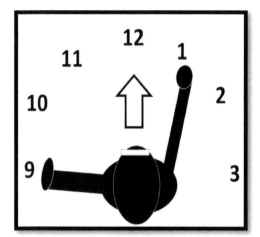

- Now imagine your hands are your mirrors.

Birds-eye view

- Turn your head to look at your left 'mirror'. Can you see your right mirror? No you can't.

- Now turn your head to look at your right mirror. Can you see your left 'mirror'? No you can't.

- Now look forward. You can just make out the edge of your left hand but can you see detail? No you can't.

- Equally, while looking forward, you can see your right mirror but you can't see detail (you can put your arms down now).

So, the left side mirrors **CANNOT** be seen while the HGV Driver is looking forward. For this reason and as a point of interest, this is why HGV Drivers call the left side of a HGV their **'Blind-Side'**. Just think about that for a moment. Even those that have passed a HGV test; are experienced HGV Drivers; that know they must and will look into the left mirrors as often as is possible still call the left side of the HGV their **BLIND SIDE**. It cannot be seen when the HGV Driver looks forwards.

If you take anything from this book I would like you to remember that.

That is why you must be 100% sure that it is safe before you move down any side of a HGV but especially the left side. The smaller the road-user you are, or the quicker you are moving (especially when you are filtering through slower moving traffic) the harder it will be for the HGV Driver to see you. Due to this 'Blind-Side' I would highly recommend you don't move down the left side of a HGV at all...but I have to be realistic, there will be times that you are able to do this. Please remember though that from the HGV Drivers' eyes to the left-side mirrors it is nearly 2 meters away. A HGV Driver must look to the left, focus, assess if anything is there (while the natural behaviour of the human eye is to react to the movement that is passing the window), then possibly look into the other two or three mirrors, each one having to be focused on and then assessed for danger, with the average time being 0.7 seconds...and as I have shown you, while all this is going on, the right side mirrors aren't being looked into as the HGV Driver physically can't look left and right at the same time.

Moreover, the ultimate goal of a HGV Driver is to move forwards, the same as you. Of course HGV Drivers will use their mirrors to look around their vehicle (it would be impossible to manoeuvre a HGV safely without using the mirrors), but at certain times there is so much going on in front of the vehicle that the mirrors may not have been looked into. The HGV Driver may be dealing with aggressive manoeuvring from another vehicle in front of them; they may be keeping an eye on a Cyclist that is ahead of them; they may be pre-empting the car pulling out of a side road; there may be traffic lights; they may be looking at each individual Pedestrian that is stood at a junction just to try and read their body language and assess whether they may be about to step into the road. The HGV Driver may never have been in that area before so they may be looking at their Sat-Navs or their smart phones' map locator; they may be looking at road signs/names…and that's what a good HGV Driver is dealing with, and yes unfortunately, the bad ones may be reading some directions given to them or talking/texting on their phone! (Annoying and frustrating as that is).

Summary

Mirrors are essential for visibility. They do offer quite a good view of the area surrounding a HGV but they only work when the HGV Driver is looking into them. As I hope I have shown you, just because you can see the mirrors you must remember that you cannot know WHICH mirror the HGV Driver is looking into. Consequently, how can you know if the HGV Driver *has* seen you at all?

PLEASE REMEMBER:

- 6 MIRRORS DO HELP BUT WILL TAKE TIME TO LOOK INTO.

- ONLY ONE MIRROR CAN BE LOOKED INTO AT A TIME.

- MIRRORS MAY BE OBSCURED DUE TO VARIABLES SUCH AS THE WEATHER.

- THE LEFT SIDE OF A HGV IS CALLED THE **'BLIND-SIDE'**.

- MOVING FAST PAST A HGV WILL MAKE YOU LESS VISIBLE.

- NOTHING TELLS YOU THAT YOU HAVE BEEN SEEN.

Blind-Spots

Blind-Spots

In the previous chapter I have shown you what and where the 6 different mirrors are, what can be seen within each and what cannot be seen. I have also highlighted that what is seen in a mirror, therefore alerting the HGV Driver of your presence, is really dependent on where the HGV Driver is looking. This is key to understanding Blind-spots as the reason they exist is because the HGV Driver may not be looking at you or does not have a clear, unobstructed, direct line-of-sight view of their close surroundings. Really, there are two types of Blind-spot.

The first type of Blind-spot is the Driver-related, **Observational Limitations**. They are caused by the HGV Driver not looking in a certain direction or mirror because they are having to look in another direction or mirror depending on the situation they are in. I have already touched on this in the 'Mirrors' Chapter (9o'clock, 1o'clock exercise) so will not repeat myself but put simply where the HGV Driver is *not* looking may mean you have not been seen.

The second type of Blind-spot is the **Physical Obstructions** caused by different parts of the HGV getting in the way of the HGV Driver's direct line-of-sight. These types of Blind-spot are either caused by the design of the HGV, its size or the nature of how HGVs move.

What you will notice is that as I speak about the Blind-spots the two types are actually intertwined. As your knowledge grows you will see that one is created by the HGV Driver trying to overcome the other. This will become clearer in the 'Positioning & Manoeuvring' Chapter but as I have been discussing the mirrors let's start with how they cause Blind-spots too.

Mirror Blind-spots

There is one major issue with HGV Mirrors.

Can you think what it might be?

They are solid lumps of plastic and glass.

They are not see-through…and

They are of considerable size.

As a result the mirrors themselves cause an obstruction for the HGV Driver. The images above show what the average view is like for a HGV Driver. Paying attention to the image on the left, you can see that the mirror blocks a portion of the road. You can also see how the Cab frame/A pillar (circled) adds to this Blind-spot. Looking at the image on the right, the obstruction is even bigger as the mirror is a lot closer to the HGV Driver. Imagine if those Pedestrians were crossing the road a metre to their left. They would be completely obscured by the mirror. As they are walking away from the HGV it is not a problem but imagine if they were walking towards the HGV; they could be missed by the HGV Driver. This is because the mirrors cast 'beams' of Blind-spot across the road and footpath.

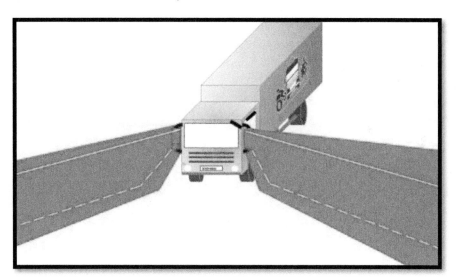

As the HGV Driver looks around their surroundings portions of the road will be obscured from view due to these beams of Blind-spot. Now most of the time these won't be an issue as the HGV Driver can see what is in front of them as the HGV moves forward.

Where it does become an issue is when the HGV is approached from the side or the HGV Driver is approaching any type of junction, turning into a side road, approaching or on a roundabout. Of course the HGV Driver should physically look around their mirrors to check but they may forget to do it as other issues grab their attention: Pedestrians on the footpath about to cross the road; traffic lights; traffic slowing down/speeding up, other road-users, the need to check the left side mirrors or, more likely, the very fact that they have seen what appears to be a clear road in front of them means they may not look. Let me explain.

The Potential Consequence of this Blind-Spot

Look at the images below. This could be a roundabout or any type of junction but for this example I will use a T-junction. The biggest danger of the Mirror Blind-spot is caused when the speeds of the Cyclist and HGV Driver interact. They don't necessarily need to be the same speed as not all junctions are at perfect right angles, they just become equal in their direction and intention (This is also a potential danger for Pedestrians crossing the road too).

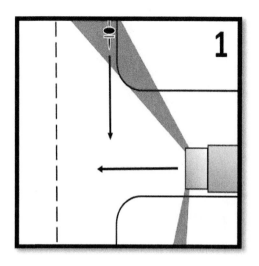

Image 1

The HGV Driver slows down for the junction and the speeds of the Cyclist and HGV Driver become equal. As the HGV Driver looks right the Cyclist is lost behind the mirror.

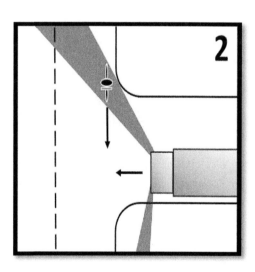

Image 2

As the HGV Driver gets closer to the junction they will look right and left but the Cyclist continues to be obscured by the mirror.

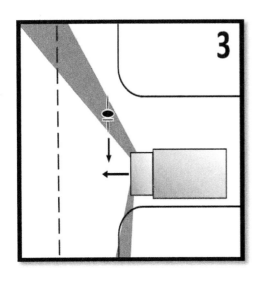

Image 3

The HGV is now at the junction. The HGV Driver may have looked around their right mirror, and to its right side but as the Cyclist moves from the HGV Driver's right to left the Cyclist may still be hidden.

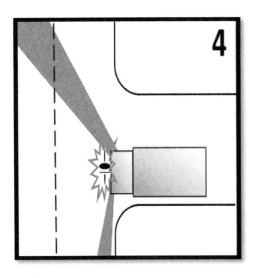

Image 4

The HGV Driver is unaware of the Cyclist. As a result the HGV Driver continues into the junction and across the path of the Cyclist.

Due to how the Cyclist remained hidden this Blind-spot is a real danger. Often, on approaching the junction, it actually looks clear to the HGV Driver. Due to your size this is a lot more relevant to Cyclists but I have lost a large van in this Blind-spot before so it really depends on the size of the junction and angle of the intersecting roads. I know it is easy to say this is an issue and you may well have priority on the road but I want you to be aware of this. I am not saying it is your fault if something happens as a result of this Blind-spot; it is the responsibility of the HGV Driver to look and I am not trying to get away from that but this book is about information and advice. I know that Cyclists have been injured and killed due to the mirror Blind-spot so I just want you to know that this is an issue and, unfortunately, looks like an issue that will remain for the foreseeable future due to the nature of HGV design.

Summary

PLEASE REMEMBER:

- MIRRORS ARE SOLID PIECES OF PLASTIC AND GLASS.

- MIRRORS ARE NOT SEE-THROUGH.

- MIRRORS WILL BLOCK THE DRIVER'S VIEW AT CERTAIN TIMES.

- THE MIRROR BLIND-SPOT BECOMES MORE OF A HAZARD WHEN THE HGV IS APPROACHING OR MANOUVERING IN A JUNCTION, AT A CROSSING OR ON A ROUNDABOUT.

Cab Blind-Spot

Cab Blind-Spot Explained

The Driver's seating area, or Cab, is responsible for the very large and very dangerous 'Cab' Blind-Spot. This is a combination of the height of the Cab and the Driver's seating position.

Imagine you are sitting on the sofa with a tray on your lap. You cannot see your feet unless you lift your legs out in front of you. If you lower them slowly there is a point at which your feet will disappear from view, behind the tray. You do not have a direct line-of-sight to your feet as the edge of the tray is blocking your view of the ground. This is a Blind-spot. It is the same in a HGV due to the dash board and the bottom edge of the windscreen. Now imagine if that same tray extended 2 metres on your left. You cannot see anything below that tray. Due to the width of the HGV Cab, this is also the same for a HGV Driver. Now imagine if you were sat on a 6ft high sofa and the same 2 meter-long tray was put on your lap. You can start to get an idea of the size of area that cannot be seen by the HGV Driver due to the height and design of the HGV Cab. Using the image below, if you can imagine the black dotted line is the edge of your tray, you can see that there is quite a substantial Cab Blind-spot around the front and side of the HGV Cab. The red/shaded area shows you what cannot be seen by the HGV Driver.

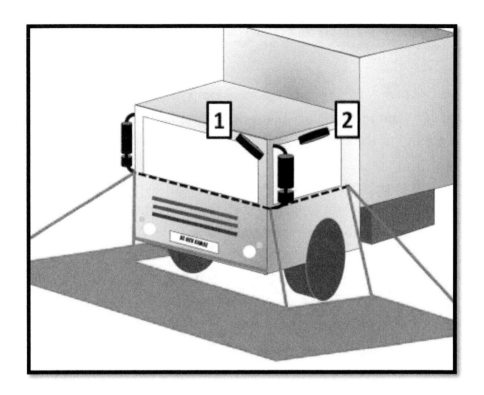

This shows how the design of the Cab and its height creates the large Cab Blind-spot. Also, the higher that Cab, then the bigger those Blind-spots will become.

Due to this large Blind-spot HGVs have been fitted with extra mirrors to try and alleviate it. As I have already shown you the different mirror views I won't repeat myself but you can see why the Front bumper mirror (1) and Close proximity mirror (2) were introduced. They are there to help the HGV Driver see into these Blind-spots…but I must make it clear again: the Driver cannot see into both of them at the same time, and they only work when being looked into.

In reality then this is what a HGV Driver will see when looking across their Cab and into their left-side mirrors. The majority of the view is actually passenger seat, passenger door, dashboard, gearbox cover and/or cab floor. Here you can really get an idea of how far the left-hand mirrors are from the HGV Driver (nearly 2 metres away in fact) and how the design of the HGV will obscure the HGV Driver's view of their close surroundings. I would like you to try another little experiment.

- Close your left eye and turn your head to the left.

- Using your right eye imagine the bridge of your nose is the edge of the left-side window.

This is how it appears when the HGV Driver looks left. While a bit simple, this gives a really quick example of what the HGV Driver sees. Their left-side, peripheral vision becomes useless as it is obscured by the internal structure of the Cab. As a result, the HGV Driver's only way of seeing their left side is via those mirrors.

There is also one variable that will change for every HGV on the road. It will definitely affect the size of the Cab Blind-Spot.

Can you think what that variable might be?

The Driver

(Well done if you got it right!)

The HGV Driver's individual height will change the size of the Cab Blind-Spot.

Using the image below let us say the white-figure HGV Driver is tall. They are 6ft/180cm +. They will have longer legs, therefore their seat will probably have to be raised for a more comfortable driving position (otherwise their knees will be more bent and the physical strength required to operate the HGV pedals becomes a lot greater). Because the seat is higher their eye-line will be higher too.

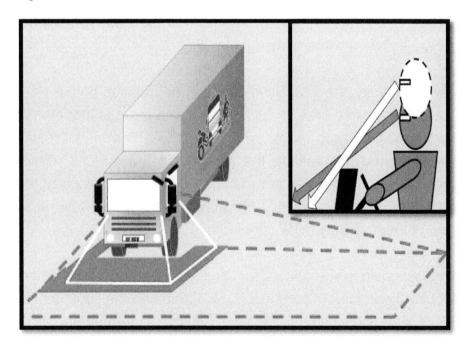

Consequently they will be able to see slightly more of their surroundings (the white lines). This Blind-spot will still exist in some form but the size of the Cab Blind-Spot will reduce, slightly.

As the red/shaded-figure HGV Driver is shorter, therefore with shorter legs, the seat will probably be lowered so that the HGV Driver can reach the pedals. As this HGV Driver is lower in the Cab so is their eye-line. The side and front Cab Blind-Spots will actually *increase* in angle and become more parallel with the ground. If you then get a short HGV Driver in one of the newer, extremely high Construction HGVs, the front, and especially the left-side Cab Blind-spot will become so large that the HGV Driver will struggle to see a car or van let alone someone as small as a Cyclist. This will affect you in as much as while you know there *is* a 'Cab' Blind-Spot on the left and front of the Cab, you will not know just *how big* that Blind-Spot might be.

Now, obviously, the Cab Blind-spot can be reduced by the HGV Driver looking into their correct mirrors. The issue is though that the Cab Blind-spot exists when the HGV Driver is looking forwards, and this will be the majority of the time. It occurs because the HGV Driver is reading the road and looking at the most likely place of potential collision, and this will always be in front of them as they move forwards.

It comes down to split seconds. I can't tell you when a HGV Driver will use these mirrors because it will depend on the situation the HGV Driver finds themselves in, but one thing to remember about HGVs, is that a lot of the time the HGV Driver will be looking forward or diagonally left out of their front windscreen. This is when the Cab Blind-spot will exist. Yes, the HGV Driver will use their mirrors but just like you the HGV Driver needs to look at the road in front of them as this is where the biggest threat of collision comes from. I have asked you to carry out that little exercise with your hands at 9o'clock and 1o'clock. This has shown you that a HGV Driver cannot see their left side mirrors when looking forwards, but in addition to this I have now also shown you that even when the HGV Driver does look left, unless you happen to be in a specific mirror at the exact second the HGV Driver looks into it there is a very good chance you may not have be seen. This is certainly more relevant to the 'close proximity' mirror as it only shows a very small area of vision. Just imagine how lucky you would have to be for me to see you in the split second I look into that mirror.

Advance Stop Lines and Bike Boxes

There is another very important concern of mine (and many others) that I want to highlight to you in relation to the Cab Blind-spot. That is the supposedly safer, cycle-friendly road design that we see on our roads. I am talking about the Advance Stop Lines (ASLs), more commonly known

as 'Bike Boxes'. If you do not know what ASLs are they are a painted box positioned in front of traffic stop lines **(1)**. These enable Cyclists to get in front of stationary traffic at junctions, the theory being that vehicle drivers will have to wait for Cyclists to move off, which decreases the chance of drivers squeezing past Cyclists and endangering them.

I understand why Cyclists would use the Bike Box. You may feel it is safer to be in front of traffic at a junction as car users can see you directly in front of them. I also understand that you may use them because that is where you think you are *supposed* to position yourselves in a

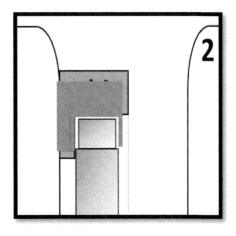

junction, as that is what the road markings are telling you. Actually you don't have to use them at all and, as you can see, the Cab Blind-spot is actually the same shape as an ASL **(2)**.

If there is a HGV already at the junction and you then ride into the ASL then you are moving directly into this Blind-spot so please keep this in mind. If, on the other hand, you are already at the junction and a HGV Driver comes up behind you, *placing you*

in their Cab Blind-spot, then you need to make a decision. Do you move left and out of the path of the HGV? If you did move to the left you will probably still be inside part of the Cab Blind-spot anyway. You could move to one side and then wait for the HGV Driver to pull away but then they should already have seen you as they will be looking to stop their HGV at the stop line and you

are already right there for them to see: you are traffic in front of them and they must wait for you to carry out your manoeuvre…like all road users must do. Or, do you stay where you are? If so I would recommend you turn around and try to make sure the HGV Driver has seen you. Make eye-contact…if possible. Give them a wave for example. Any competent HGV Driver will understand the reasons why you are doing it. Maybe signal to them what your intentions are. Are you going straight or turning? You may feel a bit of an idiot doing it but I know I would be grateful for the information if I were sat behind you in my HGV. The intentions of Cyclists are not always very clear so it can't hurt to let the HGV Driver know what you're going to do (If it isn't clear I regularly lower my window and ask Cyclists where they are going, just so I know). Another option could be to possibly move further forwards so you are in front of the Cab Blind-spot. The problem you may then be faced with is does the actual junction allow you to do this? You don't want to move so far forward that the flow of traffic across your front then endangers you.

You do have to have a bit of a debate with yourself. Ultimately, you are a road user and you are in front of the HGV so the HGV Driver does need to allow you to carry out your manoeuvre first. Being in front of the HGV means the HGV Driver should do this. As I have said above, if the HGV Driver has approached you from behind then they will have seen you. Just be careful not to ride into the Front portion of the Cab Blind-spot when a HGV is already stationary at a junction.

I would recommend you don't pass through the Cab Blind-spot but I have to be realistic. There will be times that you will be moving faster than congested or stationary traffic, and after all, that is one of the advantages of riding a bicycle. But, I would highly recommend you don't enter the Cab Blind-spot at any type of junction. You cannot know where the HGV Driver is looking, or their height, so you cannot know just how big the Cab Blind-Spots are. Even if you think you know the HGV Driver's intentions it will always be safer to stay at the rear of the HGV.

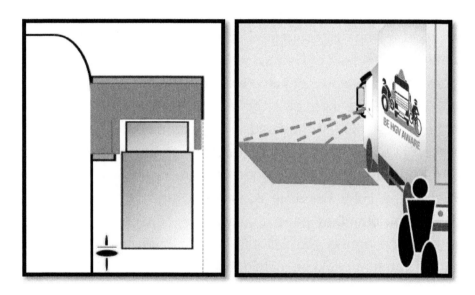

As shown in the images above, positioning yourself at the rear is the best place to be if in a junction with a HGV. The image shows you positioned on the Left side but this can equally be on the right as well depending on your intentions. You will be nowhere near the Cab Blind-spot and far enough away from the rear tyres to alleviate potential danger. The HGV Driver can also see you clearly in either their Main or Wide-angle mirrors, when they look. By stopping here you may even stop other Cyclists from entering the Cab Blind-spot if they decide to ride down the 'Blind-side' of the HGV.

With my Cyclist head on I would rather see the HGV disappearing away in front of me so would position myself here and only move *with* the HGV, staying just behind the rear but that is down to you. Equally though, when driving my HGV I would rather let the Cyclists that are surrounding me move off first so as not to risk collision. This will also depend on the fluid nature of the road. Is the road ahead still congested after the junction? Does it really matter to get ahead of Cyclists when I'm only going to be moving a few meters forwards or just crawling at 5mph? Conversely, that is worth thinking about as a Cyclist too: Do you really want to be in front of a HGV if the road in front is clear? The HGV will probably be able to move faster than you so would you then want a HGV driving behind you when you are cycling at 10-20mph? Even if the HGV Driver is considerate and is happy to drive behind you until they have a safe enough space to over-take (I know some aren't) you will still have a loud, very large HGV behind you that could be intimidating.

So it is difficult to say what you should definitely do. Ultimately, If you are at the rear of the HGV it significantly reduces the chance of collision so I know I positon myself here when in junctions with HGVs. However, if you are near the Cab please, never just set off on the assumption that you have been seen. It may not be the case.

The Cab Blind-spot and Side Roads

Keep the Cab Blind-spot in mind if you are joining from a side road too. I regularly see Cyclists pop out onto a main road as they have chosen to filter down the inside of joining traffic. I would guess some Cyclists may feel they are staying on the left and are small enough to not affect the flow of traffic on the main road due to their size. You may do this all the time as the smaller size of cars will allow you to join the main road without causing an issue. Depending on the width of the road and then with a HGV on that main road though, there may not be enough space for you both to be on the same road, in the same space and at that same time.

There is very little chance of you being seen if you do this type of manoeuvre as you are hidden by the queuing traffic but as I have also discussed, there are already Mirror Blind-spots that continuously move across the road. In combination with the Cab Blind-spot, and as your speeds interact, you may be moving straight into these Blind-spot areas as the HGV Driver looks forwards.

Look at the images below for an example of this situation.

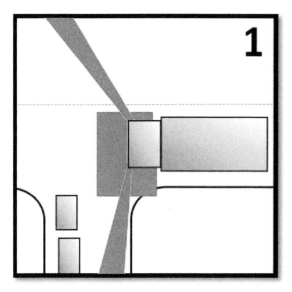

Image 1

The HGV is moving along a main road. The HGV Driver knows they have priority over all joining traffic from the side road but will still look to try and judge the intentions of the first vehicle

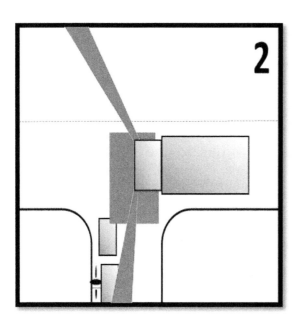

Image 2

As the HGV Driver gets closer to the junction they will have seen that the first vehicle is not intending to pull out but the movement of the Cyclist may be obscured by the queuing traffic.

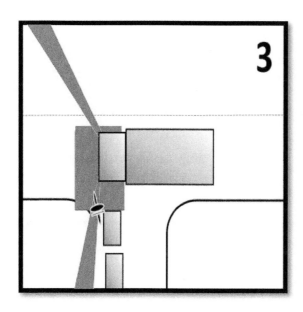

Image 3

The HGV Driver is now at the junction and as a result will probably feel they are safe to continue to move forwards. The Cyclist is now in the Mirror Blind-spot and moving into the Cab Blind-spot.

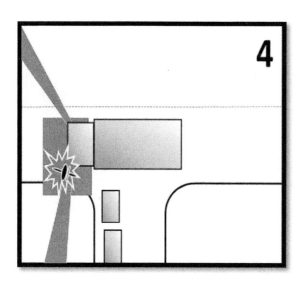

Image 4

The HGV Driver is unaware as the Cyclist enters the Cab Blind-spot which may lead to a collision.

Right-side Cab Blind-spot

Above I have discussed the Left and Front Cab Blind-spots, but you may have noticed that in the images there has been a smaller red/dark area on the right-side of the Cab too. While the HGV Driver is seated closer to the Right-side door, and they have a less obstructed view of their right side, there is still a small area that the Cab obstructs.

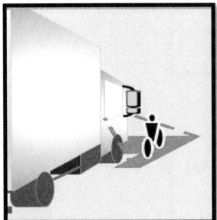

Again, this exists when the HGV Driver is looking forward. This Blind-spot will also be affected by the HGV Driver's physical height. While it stands alone as a Blind-spot its danger is increased when in conjunction with the 'beam' of the Right-side Mirror Blind-spot. While you know this Blind-spot exists you cannot know how big it might be or where the HGV Driver is looking.

The main reason I want you to know about the Right-side Cab Blind-spot is that having shown you the Left-side Blind-spot you may have thought that the safer place would be on the right, next to the HGV Driver. I just want you to know there is still a chance you will be missed if you are in close proximity to the right side of the Cab. Equally, let's say the HGV is turning left. You have moved down the right side of the HGV as you know the left side (the 'blindside') is more dangerous. As the HGV Driver knows there is an increased danger of hitting something on the left there is a very real chance that they will not be looking at the right of their vehicle during the manoeuvre because they want to be 100% sure that nothing is moving down their left side. I know that this is easy to say and of course the HGV Driver must look out for everyone but the HGV Driver cannot look in two opposite directions at the same time, and as I mentioned in the introduction, if it comes down to *your* decision I want to you to have the information that will keep you safer. I know that Cyclists have died as a result of being on the right, front corner during a left turn so I say again, the safest place to be with a HGV at any type of junction is at the rear. I will discuss this situation further in the 'Positioning & Manoeuvring' Chapter but for the moment you now know what the Cab Blind-spot is (woohoo!).

Low Entry/Direct Vision HGVs

To try and overcome the potential danger of the Cab Blind-spot there are new-ish HGV designs that are making their way into the market and onto our roads. I say new-ish because while HGV manufacturers are now starting to provide Low entry/Direct Vision (L.E/D.V) Cabs they have existed for a number of decades now. Originally they were seen on airport service HGVs that needed to manoeuvre quite close to or alongside aircraft. They have also been adopted for refuse collection vehicles. I'm sure you have seen them.

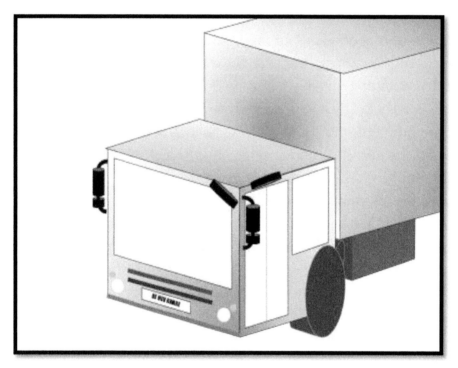

While they do improve close visibility, their original introduction for the refuse industry was due to medical conditions. The constant jumping down from a standard, high Cab by the crew was found to compress the lower spine and lead to back injuries. Couple that with lifting bins/bags of rubbish all day and you can see why operators wanted a low entry, one step-up Cab.

One of the benefits of this type of vehicle though is the massively reduced front and side Cab Blind-spots by the almost complete removal of the height...which is great! These vehicles do offer a much safer view for the HGV Driver and, therefore, a much safer HGV for other road-users in an urban environment. There are a lot of cycling road safety groups that seem to think this design will be the silver bullet that stops collisions between Bicycle and HGV but I would be cautious as they may make other road users believe they will always be seen.

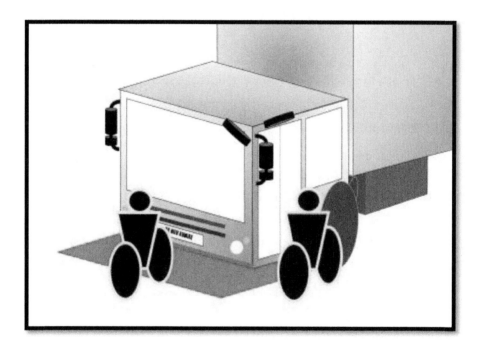

As I have said, they do offer a much safer HGV however:

- Refuse HGVs are still involved in road traffic collisions.

- L.E/D.V Cabs still require the HGV Driver to look in one direction and that will always leave the opposite side unseen.

- L.E/D.V Cabs are fitted to standard HGV chassis so they remain the same width as any HGV you see today. This will mean the left-side remains the 'Blind-side'.

- Due to the vast amounts of glass, and based on personal experience, they do suffer from an increased exposure of reflections within the Cab, in turn obscuring the mirrors.

- There are still the Mirror Blind-spot 'beams' that sweep across the road. This is because the mirrors are still the standard plastic and glass that are fitted to HGVs now.

Another point for you to think about related to L.E/D.V Cabs, is how do you know the Cab is different? If you are approaching a HGV from the rear then the back of the HGV will look the same as any other HGV. Now you can probably assume that a refuse HGV has a L.E/D.V Cab but how do you tell if any other type of HGV is a L.E/D.V HGV? Would you decide to ride along the 'Blind-side' of the HGV, and towards the Cab Blind-spot, hoping that it *might* be a L.E/D.V Cab!? Great if it is but what if it's not? That is why I want you to know that, except for the Cab Blind-spot, the same potential dangers that surround a standard HGV will also surround a L.E/D.V HGV.

One other point I would like to raise is that there already exists a vehicle on our roads that are L.E/D.V. They are low, they have *lots* of glass yet they are involved in more collisions on our urban roads than HGVs…

Can you think what it might be?

The Bus

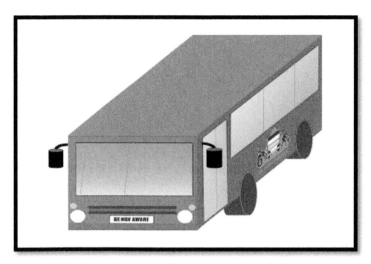

As you can see the standard local bus is similar to the L.E/D.V Cab.

- The Driver is low.
- The passenger door is completely glass.
- The Bus Driver is surrounded by enormous amounts of glass.

Yet, according to the *Reported Road Casualties of Great Britain 2011, 2012, 2013, 2014, 2015* and *2016,* in an urban environment, Buses/Coaches have been involved in more collisions than HGVs each year. Now I completely understand that these collisions tend not to be fatal when compared to HGV and Bicycle but I think it is fair to say that just because we fit Low Entry/Direct Vision Cabs onto HGVs this will not mean we will see a complete removal of collisions between HGV and

Year	Bus/Coach Collisions	Killed	HGV Collisions	Killed
2011	382	1	257	14
2012	355	6	254	12
2013	325	5	231	12
2014	310	1	270	12
2015	262	3	243	12
2016	239	2	192	10

Collisions between Bicycle and stated vehicle on **urban roads only**. Sourced from the UKs annual *'Reported Road Causalities of Great Britain'.*

Bicycle…unfortunately. They will be a *massive* improvement and I am not trying to take away just how important they are for the future of HGV design but, going back to the 9 o'clock 1 o'clock exercise, the width of the vehicle will always mean the HGV Driver will look in one direction and not be able to look in another. That is why I still want you to know what the visual limitations of HGV Drivers are, even with a L.E/D.V Cab.

This Cab design will be safer. It will reduce collisions because the front and side Cab Blind-spot is reduced, and importantly if you happen to be hit by one, you will be pushed *aside* rather than *under* the HGV and away from its tyres because the bumper is a lot closer to the ground, so despite the concerns I have raised above I must say I know I would much rather drive a L.E/D.V HGV in an urban environment when compared to a standard HGV Cab, and definitely when compared to the even higher Construction/Tipper HGVs that exist today. I think the advantages of a L.E/D.V are being recognised by quite a few HGV Drivers and logistics/distribution companies as these Cabs are becoming a lot more common on our roads, and not just on refuse HGVs.

Summary

PLEASE REMEMBER:

- HOW MUCH OF THE CAB SURROUNDINGS CANNOT BE SEEN.

- THE CAB BLINDSPOT EXISTS A MAJORITY OF THE TIME DUE TO THE DRIVER HAVING TO LOOK FORWARDS.

- THE CORRESPONDING MIRRORS DO ELIMINATE THE CAB BLIND-SPOT BUT WILL ONLY BE LOOKED INTO DEPENDING ON THE MANOEUVRE, THE SITUATION AND ONLY FOR SPLIT SECONDS.

- THE HIGHER THE CAB, THE BIGGER THE CAB BLIND-SPOT.

- THE DRIVER'S INDIVIDUAL HEIGHT MAY INCREASE THE SIZE OF THE CAB BLIND-SPOT ON THE LEFT, FRONT *AND* RIGHT OF THE CAB.

- FOR THE HGV DRIVER TO SEE YOU THE SAFEST PLACE TO POSITON YOURSELF IS AT THE REAR AND SIDE OF THE HGV.

(I must add a caveat here. Depending on the type of road or size of the lane you are in, it may be safer to actually 'take the lane' as Cycling Instructors would say. From the point of view of the HGV Driver, they can see you if you are positioned at the rear and to the left or right of the HGV. The problem is this position may not help you with regard to the vehicle that is then behind the HGV. If you are on a small roundabout or junction it may be safer to stay in the centre of the lane to stop other vehicles from over-taking you. The issue for you if you do decide to take the lane behind a HGV is that you will definitely not be seen by the HGV Driver).

Trailer
Blind-spots

The Trailer Blind-spots

The trailer on a HGV is an integral part of the HGV's make-up. Ultimately, this is where the load will be stored. The majority of HGVs that you will encounter in the urban environment will have a very high box designed to carry their load. As the picture shows, the rear of a HGV cannot be seen by the HGV Driver when the vehicle is moving forwards. I was recently driving on a very straight road so using my mirrors I tried to see how far behind my trailer I *couldn't* see. All you need to know is that it was vast! HUNDREDS of meters that I could not see behind me in my lane. I have already mentioned this in relation to 'taking the lane' above but I wanted you to know just how big the rear Blind-spot can be.

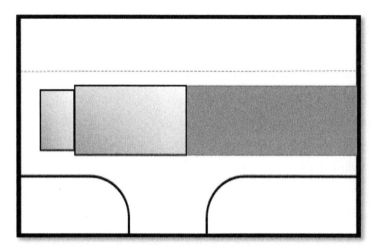

Increasingly though rear-facing cameras are becoming common on HGVs. The issue you have is you cannot know if the HGV has them (some HGVs do have stickers telling you they have cameras but these tend to be in the Cab and forward-facing for insurance reasons). Another issue is that you won't know where the camera is mounted. Some may be mounted on the top of the trailer 'box' so the Driver can see how close objects become to their rear bumper when reversing: think of it as a birds-eye view, but this will only show a few metres. Others may be mounted at bumper height and look out across the road. Both require screens and may only be operated by the activation of the reverse gear.

Others may be switched on by the HGV Driver but you cannot know if it is switched on. You may ask yourself: why is it not just turned on all the time? The problem is that at night a screen acts as a bright light within the Cab. I would imagine all of us have seen a room at night with TV light glowing through the curtains or even seen the glow of a mobile phone in a car. A screen in the Cab acts in the same way and can become a distraction for the HGV Driver.

One issue that is also relevant to rear-facing cameras and screens is that, as I have shown you, the HGV Driver already has to look forward while driving, plus they have two side windows: one on the left and one on the right. They also have 6 mirrors. A screen will add something else to look at...and remember: if the HGV Driver is looking into a cameras TV screen then they are not looking into any of their mirrors or looking at their forward and side surroundings. This means the HGV Driver can't see you. Furthermore, there is no regulated position of where the screen must be positioned. I have seen a retractable screen that appears from the top of the dash board, just to the left of the steering wheel. I have seen them mounted very low on the centre console. They have been mounted high and centrally just below the ceiling of the Cab and also right on the other side of the Cab above the passengers' door. So even if there is a camera with a screen you cannot know how easy it is for the HGV Driver to see it.

As a result of the above I want you to say to yourself: 'if I am positioned right behind a HGV I can't be seen'. If the HGVs reversing lights suddenly come on and you're sat directly behind the HGV then you probably haven't been seen. I have shown you throughout the book that just because the HGV has mirrors it doesn't mean you have been seen. Regarding the rear Blind-spot though, this *is* the one situation where the 'IF YOU CAN'T SEE MY MIRRORS I CAN'T SEE YOU'…stickers do come into effect. Be careful not to get too close to the rear of a HGV.

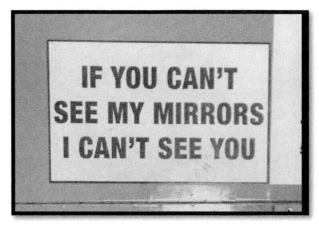

Articulated HGVs

Another Blind-Spot caused by the trailer can be found on the Articulated version of HGVs. These are the larger types of HGV that you tend to see on the motorways, though many operators do send them into the urban environment which I hope changes soon. They have a separate 'Unit' (Cab) and long trailer which 'articulates' near the front. They still have the same number of mirrors and the same Mirror and Cab Blind-spots discussed in pervious chapters. Where they differ from 'Rigid' HGVs is that the Articulated HGV Unit/Cab turns separately so therefore the view in the mirrors may either show nothing of use or may become completely filled with the view of the trailer (see image below).

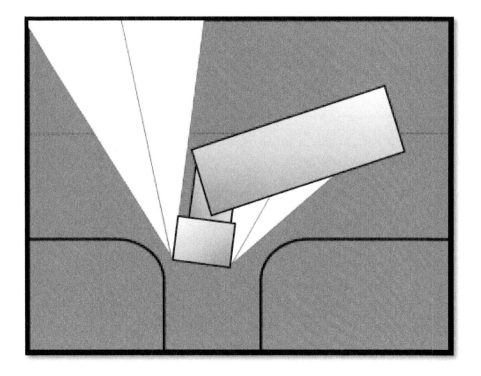

This will depend on how severe the turn is but as a rule the mirrors on the inside of the turn may be filled with only a view of the trailer, so will not allow the HGV Driver to see anyone moving down the inside of their vehicle. The mirror on the outside of the turn will show some surroundings but not the side of the HGV. There is a great video available. It is on a popular video viewing website that 'You' can find by searching 'HGV blind spot' (I didn't have permission to use their name!).

If you do watch it you will see that the Cab is slightly off centre. This may occur as the HGV Driver starts to turn but is then stopped from doing so. I know this is showing Cyclists but Motorcyclists and even Pedestrians on the footpath will not be seen either. There is also a chance a car may be lost as well.

If you cannot see it the video basically shows a Point-Of-View video footage of a HGV Driver sat inside an Articulated HGV Cab. While sat inside the Cab the Driver/camera operator zooms in to show the mirrors on the left hand side of the HGV. Both the Main and Wide-angle mirrors are empty, they show nothing in them except road. The Driver/camera operator then climbs down from the Cab, walks around the front of the HGV and reveals that the whole of the left side of the HGV is filled with Cyclists. When showing this video in my workshops there is always a very prominent gasp from the audience...which is understandable.

If you do encounter an Articulated HGV at a junction, bend or roundabout then please allow it room to manoeuvre. There is a very good chance you will be in a Blind-Spot created by the turning front Unit/Cab and trailer. I will further discuss Articulated HGVs in the 'Manoeuvring & Positioning' chapter with a few more specific examples.

Summary

PLEASE REMEMBER:

- THE TRAILER/BOX BLIND-SPOT WILL EXIST ON THE MAJORITY OF HGVS.

- THE TRAILER BLIND-SPOT IS MASSIVE IN SIZE ON A STRAIGHT ROAD.

- HGVS MAY HAVE REAR-FACING CAMERAS BUT YOU WILL NOT KNOW IF THEY ARE THERE, IF THE HGV DRIVER IS USING THE SCREEN OR IF THEY ARE WORKING.

- ON ARTICULATED HGVS THE HGV DRIVER'S VIEW MAY BE OBSCURED BY THE TRAILER IF TURNING.

- KEEP THE TRAILER BLIND-SPOT IN MIND IF 'TAKING THE LANE' BEHIND A HGV.

Blind-spots Summary

Those are the Blind-spots. This isn't meant to scare you but as you have seen they are the main danger for you as a Cyclist when interacting with HGVs. They are numerous. They exist in different forms at different times. They will change every few seconds and at least several separate Blind-spots will exist at any one moment on most HGVs. The problem you have is that you don't know which ones will exist when you encounter that HGV.

Whether what exists at that specific time is a Physical Obstruction Blind-spot caused by the HGV design or a Driver-related, Observational Limitation Blind-spot, what is key to understanding Blind-spots is that they constantly change, or more appropriately, they will change as quickly as the HGV Driver moves their head. They are caused by where the HGV Driver *IS NOT* looking. I don't mean it's because they are distracted by a phone or Sat-Nav or written directions (though they might be). I mean it is because a HGV Driver cannot see in all directions or all their mirrors at the same time. It is physically impossible for a HGV Driver to do this and I hope I have put that across to you.

What this does mean though is that while you are filtering through traffic the HGV Driver will be looking in various directions to try and alleviate their Blind-spots. This is where you may in fact move from one Blind-spot into another. Yes, the design of the HGV does mean there are physical obstructions stopping the HGV Driver from seeing you but, you may be in one Blind-spot caused by where the HGV Driver is *not* looking and then enter another as they change where they *are* looking. This does not mean the HGV Driver is not trying to alleviate their Blind-spots, in fact, Blind-spots will be caused by the HGV Driver *trying* to alleviate other Blind-spots. This means they may be looking where they feel they need to look at that specific time… you just may not be where the HGV Driver is looking.

Imagine how quickly I can move my head to look into my various mirrors versus how quickly you might be riding your bicycle. Each time I move my head I am looking into a mirror for approximately 0.7 seconds (maybe longer if the situation allows but that is the average time all drivers look into vehicle mirrors).

The Potential Consequence

Imagine my vehicle is moving along in traffic, say 10-15 mph. I have been looking forward as I have been watching the traffic in front of me. I see some movement in my Right mirror so on this occasion I decide to look right…

I LOOK RIGHT, into my Main mirror and cannot see my Left mirrors due to the width of the HGV (remember the 9 o'clock 1 o'clock exercise) so I will not see you cycling along my Left/Blindside. I also cannot see the close-front of my Cab (the Cab Blindspot). My left eye peripheral vision can make out what is happening through my windscreen, in front of my HGV, but this will be general movement rather than detailed vision. You continue to move forwards. 0.5 to 1 second later I move my head…

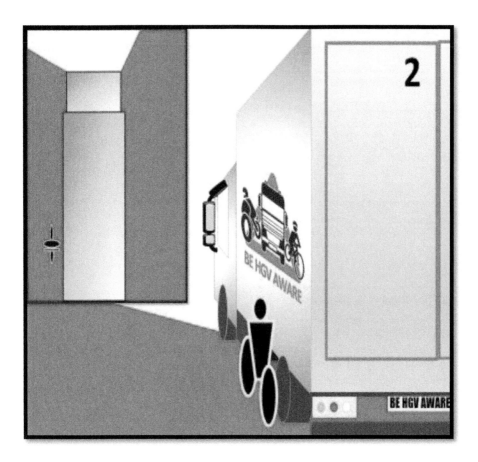

I LOOK FORWARD, through the part of the windscreen that is directly in front of me. I scan left, across the whole width of the windscreen looking in the near, middle and far distance to judge speed and direction of others, and potential hazards. I still cannot see my Left mirrors or you cycling along my left side. My left eye peripheral vision can see the left window but I cannot see the close, left side and front of my Cab (Cab Blind-spot). I can no longer see the right side of my vehicle but my right eye peripheral vision can see through the centre of my windscreen. I do not need to look into my Front bumper mirror as I am moving forwards and have seen there is no-one about to become that close to my HGV (if I were stationary or slowly passing a Pedestrian crossing I would use this mirror). 1 to 2 seconds of looking through my windscreen my eye-line is now looking through the left side of the HGV windscreen. You continue to move forwards. I turn my head to look up…

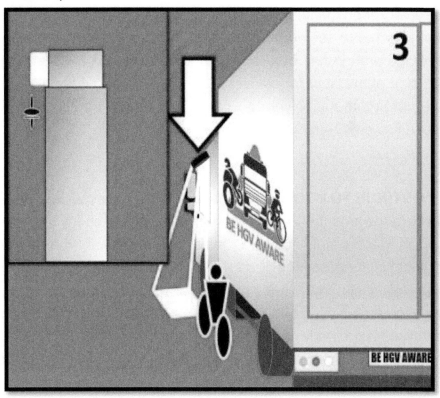

I LOOK UP and left, into my Close proximity mirror (see arrow above). The reason I do this is because I know I haven't looked left for a few seconds now so want to make sure there is no-one in the most dangerous position: in my left-side, Cab Blind-spot.

This mirror is directly over my left shoulder and nearly 2 meters away. As a result, I cannot see the close, front of my Cab and I still cannot see the left side of my HGV. My right eye peripheral vision can see through my windscreen but only the left portion of my windscreen. I definitely cannot see the right side of my HGV. Because the Close Proximity mirror is so high and does not actually allow me to see much of my surroundings this can only be a very short glance. Like I said earlier, you will need to be very lucky for me to see you in that mirror. That glance will probably average around half a second as I know I haven't checked the left side of my HGV for several seconds now. Unfortunately you are not in that mirror yet so I cannot see you. You continue to move forwards. After approximately half a second…

I CONTINUE TO LOOK LEFT but now I move my eye-line slightly forward towards the large *Main* mirror first to check my left side (which you are now not in). I cannot see the close, front of my Cab but I cannot see the close left-side of my Cab now either. My right eye peripheral vision can now see the left and centre of my windscreen but, again, this will be general movement rather than detailed vision. As I have looked into my Main mirror first I have missed you (because you are moving forwards and because it doesn't allow me to see straight down). I have scanned down the length of the Main mirror and quickly drop my eye-line into my Wide-angle mirror (below image). Unfortunately you have now passed this mirror too.

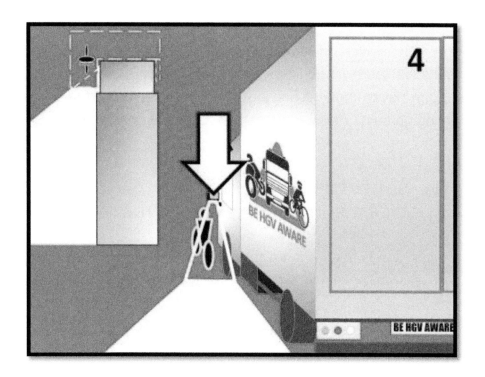

I am now under the impression that my left side is clear so I turn my head to the right to look forwards again. As I do this I see you in my peripheral vision as you pop out of my left side/front Cab Blind-spot. I then cr#p! myself because I realise that I have missed seeing a Cyclist purely because I looked right first rather than left (on this occasion). You may say, 'Well, why didn't you look left first then?', and that is what's key to understanding Blind-spots: where the HGV Driver looks is completely up to them based on conscious, subconscious and habitual reasons. You don't know where the HGV Driver is looking. If I had looked left first then I may have seen you, which is great, but I may not have seen the Cyclist, Motor-cyclist, Scooter rider or car traveling at speed along my right side.

As a HGV Driver I must be looking out for everyone and that means that there will be times you may just be missed. Ultimately, you can never know where the HGV Driver is looking because nothing on a HGV tells you that the HGV Driver has seen you.

PLEASE REMEMBER:

- SEVERAL BLIND-SPOTS EXIST ALL THE TIME.

- YOU MAY MOVE FROM ONE TO ANOTHER AS THE DRIVER LOOKS AROUND THEIR HGV.

- YOU CANNOT KNOW WHICH EXISTS AT ANY MOMENT (because)

- THEY ARE DRIVER-DEPENDENT.

- THEY ARE VEHICLE-DEPENDENT.

- THEY ARE SITUATION-DEPENDENT.

- NOTHING ON THE HGV TELLS YOU THAT YOU HAVE BEEN SEEN.

The example I have used above shows me driving my HGV in a straight line and not seeing you. While worrying for me, it hasn't meant that you have been put in immediate danger as the HGV isn't making any type of manoeuvre. Where it does become a danger to you is when I am about to carry out a manoeuvre of some kind but then miss you. I will discuss this in the next chapter.

There you are: Mirrors and Blind-spots. I told you it would be exciting (!) I hope you feel like you have learnt something about HGVs and I know, having read up to this point, you now have a greater understanding of the visual limitations surrounding HGV Drivers. As you can see there are quite a few different reasons that the Blind-spots exist, and when placed together you can start to see just how much of the HGV's close surroundings can be obscured. The Mirrors are there to help but can cause obstructions. The Cab height, while allowing the HGV Driver to judge the road conditions quite far ahead of them, actually means that anything in close proximity to the Cab can be missed. The HGV Drivers' own height can increase Blind-spots. If the HGV Driver is looking forwards then not much of their surroundings can be seen, and remember that you are small. Combine all of that with you not knowing where the HGV Driver is looking means that the potential for you being missed is actually quite significant.

I bet you can't wait to get back on our roads! But in all seriousness this isn't meant to scare you off the road. This is giving you the information I set out in the beginning of the book to make your road experience just a bit safer.

We are only half way through what I want to show you. You now have a new knowledge about HGVs and because you do I can show you some specific interactions you may have with HGVs…which will make a lot more sense now you are becoming HGV aware.

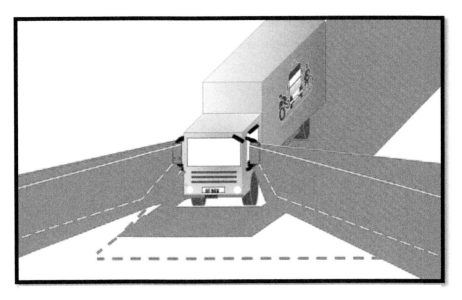

Existing Blind-spots when the HGV Driver looks forwards

HGV Positioning and Manoeuvring

HGV Positioning

In this chapter I am going to talk about the positioning and manoeuvring of HGVs, and how this affects your safety. I have already shown you the visual limitations of the HGV Driver but I want you to now understand how they affect you as the HGV is manoeuvring. This is key to increasing your safety and decision-making. The manoeuvring HGV is the biggest risk to you as a Cyclist because any manoeuvre will mean that the HGV Driver's attention is being divided between getting their HGV into a different position; looking around their HGV Blind-spots by checking various mirrors and at the same time looking for other road users entering the manoeuvring area. This is where the attention-absorbing urban environment may overload the HGV Driver's cognitive ability. Consequently there is much more chance of you being missed and becoming involved in a collision.

I have mentioned in the 'Blind-spots' chapter that the biggest risk of collision for any HGV Driver is at the front of their vehicle. This is the case when the HGV is moving forwards but obviously when that HGV has to move around obstacles, and change direction, the risk of collisions while still existing at the front now also exist at the sides and even the rear of the HGV. As a result a manoeuvring HGV poses a significant danger to you as a Cyclist.

Positioning

The first subject I want to discuss is that of positioning. HGV Drivers often position their HGV to make sure the manoeuvre they are about to carry out, or the obstacle they are about to negotiate, will be as safe as they can make it. To do this the Driver will position their HGV differently to most other road-users and the main reasons for this are:

- Defensive Driving techniques (the need of the HGV Driver to make it as safe as possible for themselves and others).

- The Required Space to manoeuvre the larger sized HGV around an obstacle.

Defensive Driving

Defensive driving is a universal driving technique that is designed to increase safety by driving in a non-aggressive, steady, sensible manner. In turn this steady, sensible manner increases any driver's ability to read the road and pre-empt other peoples' actions rather than being surprised and having to react at the last second. For a HGV Driver this ideally means slow acceleration, steady gear changes (if manual), travelling at speeds that are safe for the surrounding environment…not necessarily reaching the speed limit as it's not a target. This means more time for observation and checking their Blind-spots, gentler braking, and less chance of the HGV Driver being surprised. Because everything is slower and more controlled the HGV Driver is able to read the road and make their road experience a lot safer for themselves and others. As I say, this is ideally what should be happening but I can't pretend that this will always be the case. HGV Drivers are taught Defensive Driving techniques and where HGV Drivers can add to these techniques is by using the size of their HGV to carry out their manoeuvres more safely. This can be done by blocking lanes in certain ways. Let me explain…

A lot of urban environment junctions, or rather the lane sizes, are just not built to deal with HGVs when they need to manoeuvre. This is dependent on the size of the junction but really I am talking about the junctions where the approach road is a single lane and suddenly opens into two or more narrower lanes, often one being a filter lane to allow turning traffic to move out of the way of the traffic going straight ahead **(1)**. Every new HGV Driver has learnt from experience that if you try and use *one* of the lanes, car users mostly, will try and take advantage of the second lane and use it to over/under-take the HGV when negotiating the junction **(2).**

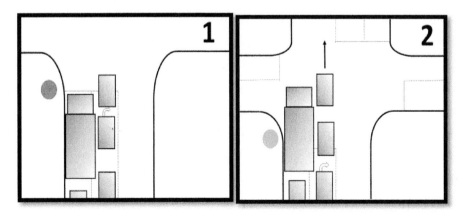

Now most of the time one or even two smaller vehicles may pass the HGV without any issue. The danger of collision occurs when the HGV is completing the junction and the road is returning to a single lane. Often cars will race forward and try to beat the HGV into the other side of the junction. One or two cars may get through but it's the third or fourth that 'follow the crowd' and try to squeeze through a fast disappearing gap that may cause a collision **(3)**. I know HGVs are slower than cars and I know it can

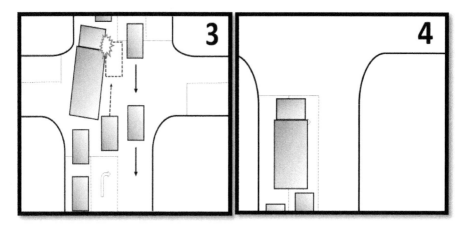

be frustrating for some but this behaviour is dangerous. When I first started HGV driving in London, and due to my inexperience, I often squeezed myself into one lane (to be courteous) but then had to take emergency action on a number of occasions. I had to swerve left (imagine if you had been on my left side?!) to make sure that no collision occurred after a car, that was too far behind my HGV, decided they were going to try and force their way past me when the gap just wasn't there anymore...and when I happened to be checking my left mirrors for Cyclists. Sometimes they got through but sometimes they didn't and they ended up with either their front wheel arch or rear bumper being ripped off against my front wheel. As a result of this behaviour by others I soon learnt that I needed to 'fill the road' as much as I could in junctions to decrease the likelihood of this happening again **(4).** Other road users may not like it but from the HGV Driver's perspective it is the safest positon to be in as it stops most vehicle users risking a dangerous manoeuvre. So, the first reason HGV Drivers position themselves differently in junctions is down to, mostly, smaller vehicle drivers potentially increasing the chance of collisions with the HGV.

Required Space

The second reason is the Required Space to physically get the length of the vehicle round an obstacle. The required space becomes relevant at any time the HGV Driver needs to change direction. The most common examples of this will be when the HGV Driver needs to carry out a left or right turn, negotiate a roundabout or reverse, but it can also occur even when there is a bend in a road.

As I am sure you are aware HGVs are very long so their wheels are positioned near the front and near the rear to make sure the HGV is nice and stable as it moves along the road **(1).** Now obviously the front wheels will dictate the direction the rear wheels move in. This is fine when moving straight as everything is in line. The issue of Required Space occurs when the HGV

Driver changes direction and the turning, front wheels are facing in a different direction to the rear wheels. As the HGV Driver turns their steering wheel obviously the fixed, rear wheels will start to move in the same direction *and* at the same time as the turning, front wheels. The problem is the rear wheels are starting from

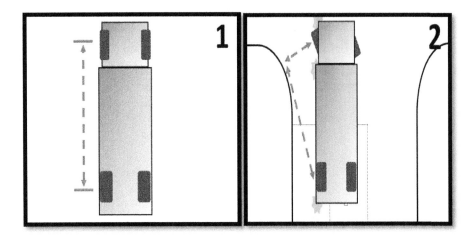

further back on the road, and are a lot further away from the obstacle than the turning, front wheels **(2)**.Consequently, if the HGV Driver was to turn too early it would mean the rear wheels will crash over the kerb and endanger any

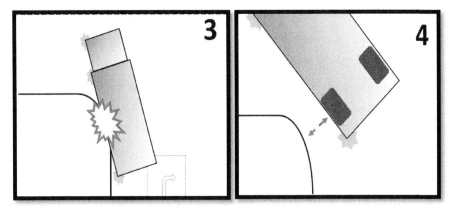

Pedestrians stood at that junction **(3)**. As a result, the HGV Driver will need to start the turn once the rear wheels are nearer to the obstacle *and also* position their HGV far enough away from the kerb to make sure the rear wheels do not endanger Pedestrians **(4)**. As a point of interest, if the HGV Driver did hit the kerb during their HGV Driving test it would be an instant fail, so you can see just how much emphasis is placed on keeping Pedestrians safe when carrying out this manoeuvre.

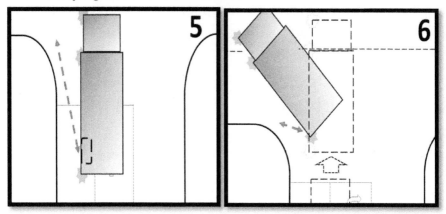

Subsequently, because the HGV Driver needs to bring their rear wheels closer to the obstacle first **(5)** the HGV will actually be driven forwards before making the turn **(6)**. This should be of concern to you as this may give you the impression the HGV is actually moving straight ahead and not turning at all. You could decide to undertake the HGV because you think the HGV Driver is going forwards when in fact they are waiting for the rear wheels to get to a point that they can start to turn **(6)**. This is a major concern related to your safety, and HGV positioning, because it creates the 'Illusion of Space'.

The Illusion of Space

In both the Defensive Driving and Required Space examples the HGV Driver is creating what appears to be space on either side of their HGV. That space is closed to cars, because that's the point, but it can look very tempting to a Cyclist as there appears to be lots of empty road on one or both sides of the HGV **(1)**. What I want to show you is that the "space" created by the HGV Driver is actually an illusion and will disappear. If you position yourself in it the chance of collision between you and the HGV significantly increases. I will explain below.

Defensive Driving and the Illusion of Space

In the example of Defensive Driving, the most common chance of collision is if you move faster than the HGV in the junction **(2).**

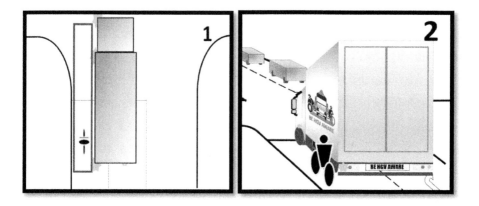

As the HGV is trying to fill two lanes (on our side of the junction) but moving into a single lane (on the other side of the junction)

the space on the left-side will disappear when the HGV passes the kerb **(3)**. Depending on how far along you are positioned on the HGV's left-side, you might suddenly find the open space now being closed to you by the position of the HGV **(4)**. If you are travelling slowly then this isn't too much of a problem as you have

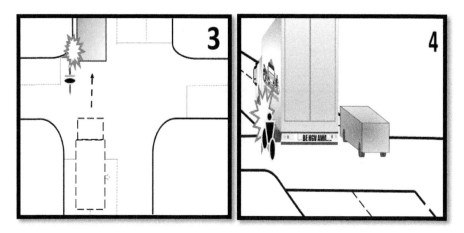

time to brake. If you are travelling at speed though, let us say because you saw the traffic lights turn green; you have seen a nice open 'space' and you started to accelerate through the lights, that space will disappear because you have the footpath directly in front of you (that may be full of Pedestrians) and the rear portion of an HGV on your right shoulder so you have no-where to go. This may lead to a collision.

Required Space and the Illusion of Space

In the example of the Required Space, again, the most common chance of collision is if you move faster than the HGV in the junction or have decided to accelerate through the junction on seeing the lights turn green **(1,2)**. The HGV Driver has created the Illusion of Space on their left. They have moved the HGV away from the kerb to carry out the left turn manoeuvre. This is to safely bring the rear wheels around the obstacle. If you are moving slowly you may have time to brake. However if you are travelling at speed because you have seen the traffic lights turn green and there appears to be a nice open space, you may be missed as the HGV Driver checks their surroundings.

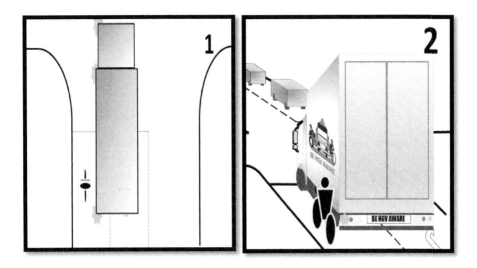

As I have mentioned above, the HGV may also appear to be going straight ahead to bring the rear wheels closer to the obstacle and that 'space' instantly disappears as the HGV Driver turns the vehicle left **(3)**. If you are in that 'space', and if you get missed by the HGV Driver in their mirror (because you may also be inside the Cab Blind-spot) there is a very real chance you will be hit by the turning HGV **(4)**.

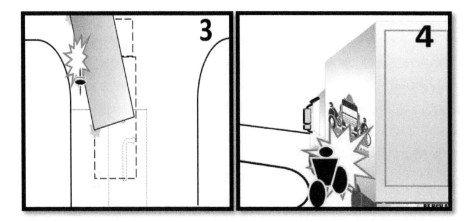

So, the reason HGV positioning should be a concern of yours is because it creates a tempting Illusion of Space that, if ridden into, can potentially increase the chance of collision between you and a HGV. However there is another reason that Cyclists may find themselves inside the 'space' created by the HGV and that comes down to a decision to undertake through slow-moving or congested traffic in junctions.

Filtering Versus Undertaking

This is where we have to touch on a delicate but very real and dangerous paradox of cycling. That is the topic of Filtering versus Undertaking.

I am saying 'undertake' above because to call it filtering may confuse. Filtering is an acceptable behaviour by Cyclists...in fact it is one of the many advantages of cycling in the congested, urban environment but it does conflict with how all motor-vehicle drivers are taught regarding the action of undertaking. In this instance, and while I am discussing HGV positioning and manoeuvring *in junctions*, I am calling it undertaking because I want to use the negative context that the term brings with it.

It is taught too and understood by motor-vehicle drivers that undertaking is a no-no on our roads. No one should undertake any vehicle unless they are completely sure it is safe to do so, for

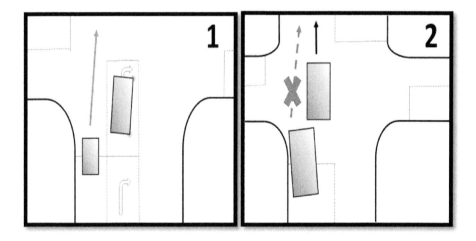

example, in a filtering junction **(1)**. I am stressing this because if you are near a HGV in a junction, and if that HGV is moving, it will never be safe to do so... that is what I keep in my head when I cycle. With my cycling head on I know that filtering is what makes cycling such a massive advantage over motor-vehicles on our congested urban roads but, I also have to remember, and I want you to remember this too, that those motor-vehicle drivers are working to a set of rules that they have been taught. One of those rules is that you do not undertake someone unless it is safe to do so. Yes, I know that another rule drivers must follow is to look out for Cyclists but please hear me out.

One of the places that motor-vehicle drivers know this 'no undertaking' rule to be in effect is in junctions **(2)**. The driver/vehicle in front has priority and must be allowed to carry out their manoeuvre before you carry out yours. If all those drivers are working to a set of rules that they know others will follow (most of the time) then it makes no sense for me as a Cyclist to ignore those rules. Yes, drivers should be looking out for Cyclists but in a junction and in an urban environment they may be moving at a slow speed so not expect faster-moving road users to pass them. They may also be looking for and reacting to brake lights, traffic lights, Pedestrians crossing the road and, yes though not great, possibly looking at mobile phones, tuning the radio or even reading a newspaper while the traffic is stationary or crawling forwards, and because they understand that the driver/vehicle behind them is following a set of rules which means they will not be undertaken, they may not take the time to look in a certain mirror just because you happen to be in that mirror. They know they have priority as they negotiate the junction so may miss you *if* you decided to undertake them in that junction.

This does come down to drivers' road training and I know some would argue that Cyclists don't have this road training. I am not about to suggest that Cyclists have compulsory road training as most have driving licenses (so actually should be aware of this conflict between Filtering versus Undertaking), and because that defeats what cycling is all about: the freedom for anyone to jump on a bike and go, but I just want you to be aware that while you have the *ability* to move past congested traffic it may not be the safest thing to do *in a junction* and especially when in close proximity to a HGV...certainly when considering all the visual limitations HGV Drivers have.

Like I mentioned in the introduction I want you to *not* rely on others for your safety. If you do decide to undertake (or filter if that's how you see it) any vehicle in a junction you are completely reliant on other people for your safety. You have surrendered your ability to stay safe. You are assuming that other road users have seen you and that *they* will keep you safe. The questions raised though are: how do you know they have seen you? So how will they then keep you safe?

I fully accept that being on the road we *have* to rely on others for our safety but that reliance is supported by our knowledge that others are following the rules of the road. If someone decides not to follow those rules, or the generally accepted behaviour, then not only does it cause frustration but it can be dangerous too. I think that is where some 'road rage' comes from: the frustration caused by others not following the agreed rules and triggering potential dangers. This may be why *some* people become so irate with Cyclists: they see them as not following the rules. I don't know why it causes such division but it comes down to people's varying knowledge, experience, empathy and personality I guess. I stand by my decision to call it undertaking though. Filtering is a massive positive of cycling in the urban environment and if you have the space then it is fine, however if you attempt it in a junction with moving traffic you are significantly increasing your chance of becoming involved in a collision.

I am not saying you shouldn't move down the inside or outside of traffic stopped at a set of traffic lights, but I want you to be safer and I just don't want you approaching a junction at speed and then undertaking other drivers that are not expecting you to do it, especially when the generally agreed behaviour is to let the person in front carry out their manoeuvre first. It just isn't safe. When it comes to undertaking HGVs though, because of your size or riding at speed *and* in combination with the HGV Blind-spots I have shown you, it becomes a lot more likely that you could be missed.

I hope you can see the logic behind my opinion. It is an opinion based on what I have seen and personally experienced as a HGV Driver of over 20 years…and as a Cyclist. It is also what I take into account when I cycle. I hope that it makes sense though. You may not agree with me and you may still think it is other people's responsibility to keep you safe at all times but we will just have to agree to disagree. I will say it again though - It makes no sense for me (when cycling) to ignore the training that the other road users have received if what I do goes against that training, and potentially increases the danger to me.

Connected to my opinion on filtering I hope you can see how that relates to the Illusion of Space. If you do decide to "filter" and then are tricked by the Illusion of Space then you are increasing the chance of collision. Just because that 'space' exists for a few seconds during a manoeuvre or even longer if stopped at a traffic light, it does not mean it will exist continually. This is another reason to position yourself at the rear of the HGV in a junction…and even 'take the lane' behind it.

This may mean that *if* you are filtering at speed as you approach a junction and that junction already has a HGV in front of you then I would ask you to slow down to allow the HGV to carry out their manoeuvre. If you decided to go for it anyway you may get through but why risk it? Is it purely because you don't want to slow

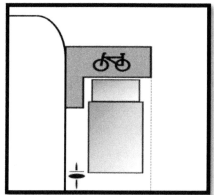 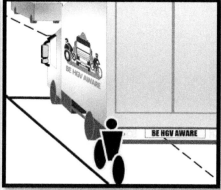

down? I know it is a pain to gain speed again, and you may have to bodge it through your gears, but it makes no sense whatsoever to try and undertake a HGV in a junction. The safest behaviour would be not to speed through a junction anyway but if you see a HGV then please allow them the time to carry out their manoeuvre first.

Without wanting to repeat myself, I know it is easy for me to say that you need to watch out for this, but the reason I am saying it is because I see Cyclists do this every time I drive in an urban environment. I see Cyclists tricked by the Illusion of Space having originally been positioned *behind* my HGV and think it is a good place to accelerate and attempt to undertake me. I then have to react to make sure that we are not involved in a collision. But, I will only react *if* I have seen the Cyclist. That Cyclist's safety has been completely put in my hands. By undertaking a moving HGV, in a junction, they are relying on me to keep them safe. They have surrendered their ability to stay safe because they have assumed they have been seen. What if I hadn't seen them though? Having seen what happens when a Cyclist is missed I do not have to try and imagine it. It is a very real image that I don't what to happen to others.

Like I said in the introduction this book is talking about if the decision is *yours* to make. If though, that decision is taken away from you because the HGV Driver over-takes you putting *you* into that 'space', or *they* attempt to get ahead of you in the junction and turn left, I completely understand your anger and frustration. I have a small mirror positioned in the end of my right handlebar to try and keep an eye on the traffic near me. I try to look out for indicators and listen for accelerating engines but that's all I can offer (Post incident I also know there are wearable forward and rear-facing cameras available too but whether any action is taken by the Police is dependent on how strong the evidence and which Constabulary you are in...though close-passing is being dealt with more and more nowadays). As a Cyclist I have had this happen to me and there is not much you can do about it I'm afraid. All I can say is, like I mentioned in the Blind-spot chapter, Cycling Instructors would say 'take the lane'. I am not a Cycling Instructor but like the HGV Driver using a Defensive Driving position to stop cars passing them in a junction, you can do the same but I accept, the concern of a HGV Driver over-taking and then 'left-hooking' you still remains a dangerous reality. Any driver and especially any HGV Driver worthy of being on the road will know what you are doing if you take the lane in a junction and will never have an issue with what you are doing...*some* might but they probably shouldn't be behind the wheel of that vehicle. Again, on the road, that's the issue we all have to deal with: people's varying knowledge, experience, empathy and personality.

Summary

If you are with or meet a HGV in a junction; if it is positioned in a way that creates the Illusion of Space; if it is your decision and you think it is a good place to undertake that HGV, I hope by reading this you have seen that potentially it is a very dangerous manoeuvre. This is because the space beside the HGV will soon disappear as the HGV Driver carries out their manoeuvre.

You now know what considerations are taken into account when a HGV Driver positions their HGV, and that the Illusion of Space will probably have been created.

PLEASE REMEMBER:

- HGV POSITIONING AND MANOEUVRING WILL AFFECT YOUR SAFETY.

- THE HGV DRIVER'S 'DEFENSIVE DRIVING' & 'REQUIRED SPACE' POSITIONING CONSIDERATIONS

- THE 'ILLUSION OF SPACE' THAT IS CREATED.

- FILTERING vs UNDERTAKING.

- YOU *COULD* UNDERTAKE THE HGV, BUT DOES IT MEAN YOU *SHOULD* ATTEMPT TO?

- DO NOT SURRENDER *YOUR* ABILITY TO STAY SAFE.

As you are becoming more HGV Aware you know the HGV Driver has numerous Blind-spots that they must check. You also now know what considerations the HGV Driver must take into account when positioning for a manoeuvre. Because the HGV is now changing direction...or manoeuvring...there are certain places that *must* be checked at certain times. What I am going to show you in the next section is if you decided to undertake the HGV during a manoeuvre, there is more chance of you being missed due to where the HGV Driver must look and how they have been trained to look around their HGV's close surroundings.

The Manoeuvring HGV

You now know what issues HGV Drivers take into consideration when *positioning* themselves for a manoeuvre. They have to think about other road users that may endanger themselves by attempting to squeeze past in a space that just isn't there. They also have to take into account the size of their HGV to manoeuvre it around whatever obstacle they intend to negotiate. But what else must a HGV Driver think about when manoeuvring their HGV?

- They must certainly not endanger Pedestrians.
- They must not endanger anyone on the road.
- They must not hit the physical environment around them for example, road signs, kerb stones, bollards etc.
- They must calculate how much space they have to manoeuvre due to the restrictions that the road design may place on them.

- They must make sure the space they are *moving into* is safe, and remains safe throughout the manoeuvre.

As you can see, that is a lot to keep in the forefront of your mind. So, the HGV Driver must position their HGV to reduce the chance of hitting the physical environment; they must position their HGV to reduce the chance of other road-users encroaching into their manoeuvring area and, they must aim to keep it as safe as they can for themselves and others. That is quite a lot to think about when driving a vehicle that doesn't allow you to see your close surroundings very well.

HGV Drivers know they must check their Blind-spots to make sure their close surroundings are clear but the problem they now have is that while they are still impaired by the ever-changing Blind-spots, the Blind-spots are worsened because the HGV Driver now needs to look in certain directions at certain times during that manoeuvre. This is where a combination of the 'Observational' Blind-spots and the 'Physical obstruction' Blind-spots can potentially become a major issue for you.

Turning

To help explain where the HGV Driver is looking...and isn't looking...and how the design of the Cab blocks the HGV Driver's direct view I am going to use the Left turn as an example. The reason I am discussing the Left turn is because it is one of the manoeuvres that has led to numerous injuries and deaths between HGV and Bicycle. I am not trying to make excuses for any HGV Driver who has ever been involved in a collision while carrying out the Left turn. I just want to offer some other explanations as to why they may have occurred, other than the belief by some that the HGV Driver just didn't look…because that is not always the case.

I know you may not have agreed with me with regards my 'Filtering versus Undertaking' argument but I am going to try and highlight the dangers to you *if* you decided to undertake a HGV in a junction. I know that not all incidents between HGV Driver and Cyclist are caused by this action but some are, and because this book is about helping *you* to stay safe I would like you to keep an open mind as you read it.

What I was originally going to show you was a very detailed, second-by-second, image-heavy description of how I would carry out a Left turn. I was going to show how I looked from one mirror or windscreen to another but after 50+ images, and about twenty pages of description, my drawings hadn't even started to show the actual turn! and because of the differing variables such as the manoeuvre being carried out, the time it takes to carry out different turns due to the size of the junction or the size of the HGV; how alert the Driver is; how alert other road-users are; how busy the junction is; how busy the footpaths are surrounding the junction or how much traffic is in front of the HGV, it didn't matter how I described *my* left turn because it doesn't mean this is how *all* HGV Drivers will do it. I recognised I just needed to give you key information and get you thinking about what is happening during a HGV turn.

I am not going to position you in any of the images either. You will see the Cyclist image in some of the images but by its nature being on the road is a very fluid existence. I want you to start to think about how you might be seen by the HGV Driver in various situations but also remembering that each look or glance by the HGV Driver is only 0.7 seconds (on average) before then looking in another direction. The HGV might be stationary; it might have just started to pull away; it might be approaching the junction at speed. You are becoming more HGV Aware with each page so I want you to think in terms of you either being the first Cyclist at the junction or you could be the 6th in a line of Cyclists approaching from behind the HGV, so think about what you might do knowing that the HGV Driver may have only used a certain mirror for 0.7 seconds. As I have shown you in previous chapters you could easily be missed as the HGV Driver looks around their surroundings so please try and think what you would do if you met this turning HGV at any moment.

Another variable to think about while reading the next section, and a reason you may be missed by the HGV Driver, is the way the human eye works. As humans we are only capable of seeing a very small, detailed area within our vision. Yes, we have peripheral vision that can pick up movement but as I mentioned earlier in this book, the HGV Driver's world is full of movement. Consequently HGV Drivers have to sometimes ignore their natural instinct to react to movement in their *peripheral* vision because they must concentrate on what their *central* vision is showing them at that precise moment. They cannot be distracted by the world moving past their mirrors as this would mean they could miss something *within* that mirror.

One other variable I would also like you to think about is my term 'attention-absorbing'. I will mention it throughout this section of the book as often it is the attention-absorbing surroundings that might mean the HGV Driver has to look a fraction of a second, or one or two seconds longer in one direction. This will mean they cannot look around their surroundings as quickly as they might want to because they are having their attention 'absorbed' in a specific direction. The urban environment can be a very busy one to drive in. Having driven in London for a number of years I was always mentally exhausted at the end of each day. I just want you to think about how much information the HGV Driver is having to process, which in itself may lead to the HGV Driver's inability to process *all* that is happening.

It is also worth commenting that HGV Drivers are conditioned by their time spent on the road, and training. HGV Drivers who have passed their License in the UK are very well trained. It took me three attempts to pass my Class 1/C+E (Articulated HGVs) license because I was not at a sufficient level. I had passed my car theory and practical; I had passed my Class 2/C (Rigid HGV) theory and practical yet the Class 1 took a bit longer. All HGV Drivers will have at least two driving licenses so have sat and passed at least two Theory tests and two practical tests. They may also have regular assessments from their employers (some may not). The reason I mention this is you must remember that one thing HGV Drivers will expect is that others follow the rules of the road, as that is what their training has told them will happen. Yes, we have all experienced times when others do not follow the rules, but if a HGV Driver is about to go through a Green light they will expect those on a Red light or Red man to follow that traffic signal. This is the training they have received and due to the amount of time spent on the roads this is also the conditioning they have become used to. No road user expects others to ignore the rules and career road users like HGV Drivers, while having to deal with the occasional flouter, know that the rules are followed by the majority. This may mean assumptions are made by the HGV Driver but they are assumptions based on the training they have received…and you would hope, people's own survival instincts.

One more thing I will quickly mention is that some HGVs have an audible message activated when the left indicator is switched on:

"WARNING!! This vehicle is turning left. WARNING!!"

If it does then please see this as a warning not to enter the 'space' on the left. If the HGV doesn't have an audible message then what I am about to discuss is even more relevant.

The Left turn…

Positioning

You already know that I have to position my HGV to try and reduce the danger of potential motor-vehicle risk-takers behind me. You can see from the picture that I have decided I need to occupy both lanes to make sure this doesn't occur and so I can get the rear wheels around the left kerb safely **(1).** While I need to block both lanes to make it safer for me, unfortunately my positioning of the HGV has created the 'Illusion of Space' on my left side…making it less safe for you *if* you move into it **(2)**. If you are approaching that HGV from behind then I want you to remember why that is space there.

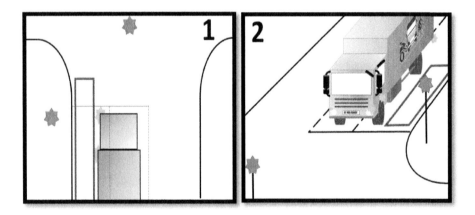

I completely understand that Cyclists will ride into this 'space' and some may position themselves in front of the HGV. I know this happens because I see it every day I drive a HGV (maybe I see it because I am 6'2" and therefore have a reduced Cab Blind-spot??). I wish it didn't happen but this is the reality on our roads. It's just seen by some Cyclists as a way of getting in front of the

HGV, unfortunately. I want to reiterate to you that you do not have to follow the supposedly cycle-safe road markings as they will lead you straight into my Cab Blind-spot. Another reason not to enter this 'space' is because you know that it is going to disappear as the HGV turns left. These are two reasons to stay at the rear of the HGV if it is making a turn.

Where *Does* the HGV Driver look?

While sat at the junction I will be using the mirrors to look around my HGV but the one obvious place I will be looking is at the traffic light. I may also be looking at the Pedestrians crossing the road. I may be looking at which traffic flow has their green light and waiting for mine to change. I may use this time to look at some directions given to me as I may not have been in the area before. This might be a written piece of paper or a Sat-Nav or even the Map application on my phone…you might not like it but I may never have been in that area or delivered to the next address before (this is a reality of being a HGV Driver: you may know your route as you ride it all the time but I may not know my day's route).

Where I look will alternate between my surroundings/mirrors, and the traffic light but the longer I'm stationary the more time I will spend looking at the traffic light because I am waiting for it to change **(3).** This is an example of when the attention-absorbing nature of the road will mean less time looking into my mirrors. This is when I may have missed you moving along my Blind-side (my left) and into the Cab Blind-spot.

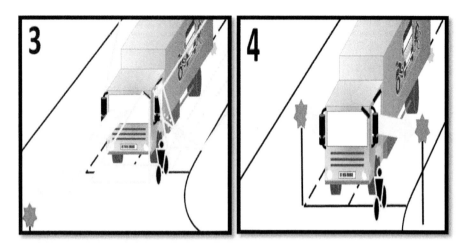

As not all junctions have traffic lights positioned, like in image number **3**, I may have to look for one to the right or left of my Cab **(4).** That's great if it is on my left as it means my concentration is already on the left and I can look into my Left mirrors more easily but, if it is on the right, then the left Blind-side mirrors will not be looked at as often. Also, if I have misjudged my stopping distance or reacted too slowly to a changing traffic light, it might mean my HGV is further forwards than I would like and I am having to crouch down in my seat to make sure I can see the light turn green. This will also mean I am not looking into my mirrors and I may have missed you on my Blind-side.

Which Mirrors and When?

This is the one variable I have tried to help you understand as the book has progressed. I cannot tell you how each individual HGV Driver will look around their surroundings because I do not know.

I know the mirrors I choose to look into and the order in which I look into them are based on my training but also my own experiences. This has developed from wanting see what is next to me but equally it has come from my own near misses. It has also come from using pictures from the media to analyse how other HGV Drivers have been involved in collisions. I know that may sound morbid but I keep an eye on the news regarding cycling deaths with HGVs. By looking where the casualty tent has been erected around a HGV I can sometimes see what may have happened. I used this information in my workshops and I am using it in this book too. Using the media images can only lead to speculation but because the details of the accident investigations are never made easily available it is often a guessing game that I hope has kept other Cyclists safer when I am in the HGV they are encountering. So looking around a HGV should be similar for all HGV Drivers but there could be certain differences based on each HGV Driver's experiences.

Because of my experiences, how I react on seeing the lights turn to Red-Amber, is to instantly look towards my left side and check all my Mirrors on that side. I then check the front bumper mirror and then scan the full width of my windscreen, being careful to look into the fore and middle ground as this is the space I am about to occupy **(5).** You must remember that while I am looking left and forwards the right side of my HGV is now a Blind-spot (remember the 1o'clock, 9 o'clock exercise).

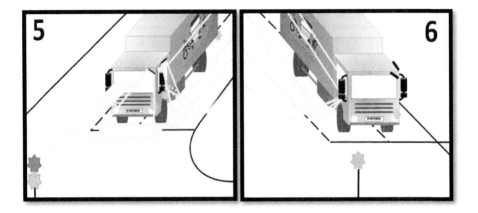

The reason I mention the right side is because I know some Cyclists use the right side because they know the left side is dangerous. I want you to know that the right side is not the safer option. Once I have checked the left and front of my HGV I will then check the mirrors on my right **(6)**. As the right-side, Main mirror is quite a large obstruction I may have missed some Pedestrians if they have still attempted to cross the road. While I have checked *in* my right mirrors I also now need to check my Mirror Blind-spot **(7)**. To do this I lean forward in my seat and look between the mirror and the Cab body (A frame) **(8).**

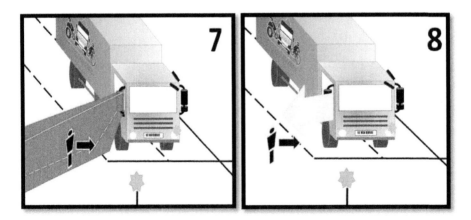

This is another example of how the attention-absorbing nature of the road can mean that I am having to look for longer in one direction and not able to look at the rest of my surroundings as quickly as I would like to. As a result my left side is now a Blind-spot a fraction longer than I would like.

If there *are* Pedestrians there I will need to watch them for a number of seconds to see what they are doing: Do they stop walking and return to the kerb? Or, do they keep walking and expect me to wait for them? Either action by a Pedestrian will mean I am not able to look at my left side at all. Depending on where you are positioned, this is another occasion where you may be missed due to the attention-absorbing nature of my surroundings.

Your Warning I am About to Pull Away

Even though the traffic lights will undoubtedly have turned green by the time I have checked all around me I cannot move off until I know it is safe to do so. This may confuse you as my HGV is not moving even though the lights are green. Once I have looked around my surroundings, and I am happy that it is safe, I will *then* release my hand break and start to pull away. When I do this you will hear a very loud P-TSSsss! **(9)**. (you won't see it!).

This is the sound of the airbrakes dumping the air that is holding my brakes on. If you have decided to move down the side of the HGV, because you think you can get to the front before it starts

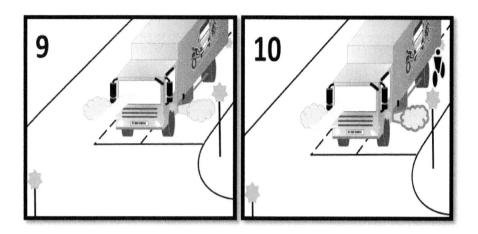

to move, then this is an audible warning signal to you that you need to slow down or stop **(10)**. Due to the numerous variables the HGV Driver might be reacting to you cannot know if that HGV Driver has seen you because you do not know where they are looking. Consequently you cannot know if they will allow you to move ahead of them…another reason to stay at the rear of the HGV.

Where *Will* The HGV Driver Look?

The one place I can tell you *all* HGV Drivers will look is the space that the HGV is turning into. This will always need to be checked and is an important part of where the HGV Driver looks during a turn. The HGV may be moving, or it may be setting off from a stationary position but the area the HGV is *moving into* must be looked at by the HGV Driver. It must be checked *while* the manoeuvre is being carried out to make sure that the space the HGV is *going* to occupy remains safe.

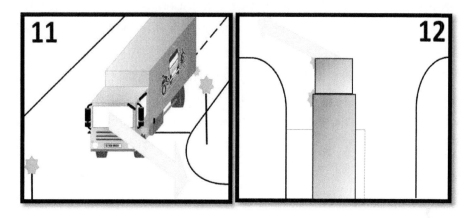

To make sure this space remains safe I will look through the left portion of my front windscreen at different times **(11).** The reason I must look diagonally through the left portion of my windscreen is because I cannot start to turn my HGV until the rear wheels are safe to start the turn (remember the 'Required Space'). My HGV will be moving in a forward direction prior to the turn so I *have* to look diagonally through the left portion of my windscreen as the HGV is still facing forwards **(12).**

At all times I am looking for potential hazards but the main hazard I will be looking for is a Pedestrian stepping out into the road. In a busy urban environment I must look out for Pedestrians as I cannot know what they are going to do **(13)** (Generally, as vehicle road users, everyone wants to be moving in the same direction. We are confined by the kerb stones or white lines and the want to move forwards. Unfortunately, Pedestrians do not have to stick within these confines. In the UK we do not have a law regarding the use of Pedestrian Crossings so they are free to cross the road wherever they want. This is not too much of an issue but for reasons unknown to me some choose to step out into the road even though they can see a vehicle coming towards them. Perhaps they believe the traffic will stop for them. Perhaps they are taking the 'Pedestrian has priority' rule for granted but whatever the reason I must now make sure I do not endanger any Pedestrians attempting to cross the road as I drive towards them.)

This means I must take a bit longer to look out for them and the attention-absorbing environment again means I cannot look around my surroundings as quickly as I might like to. If I am looking out for Pedestrians in front of me though, it means I cannot look for you in my mirrors **(14)**.

One other factor related to this is what this might look like to you when I do look diagonally into this space.

If you are positioned behind my HGV you might decide to use my left mirror to see what I am doing **(15)**. You might see me looking towards my left and it may appear to you that I am looking into the mirror **(16)**: my head is turned the same way and my eye-line would appear to be the same as if I were looking in that mirror. It would make sense that you could assume I have seen you. Unfortunately I am not looking into that mirror because I am looking diagonally left, and past it. Again, that is another time you may be missed.

Are You Obscured by Traffic?

I have mentioned a few times now about how the HGV Driver will probably position their HGV to make it as safe for *them* as possible during a turn. This is quite common when there are two lanes at a junction as it allows the HGV Driver space to manoeuvre safely **(17)**. You already know that this positioning can pose a danger to you as it creates the Illusion of Space but you might be thinking 'but the HGV Driver can still look in their left mirror before they manoeuvre'. You are right, they can but there are times when the HGV Driver's view may be obscured by the traffic behind them. So far the examples I have used throughout the book show one HGV in an empty junction with you approaching them from behind but let's add a bit more reality here. Imagine if that road was filled with other traffic, which isn't hard to do. I have positioned my HGV to stop other vehicles from under or over-taking me in the junction but the view in my mirrors is now obscured by this traffic **(18).**

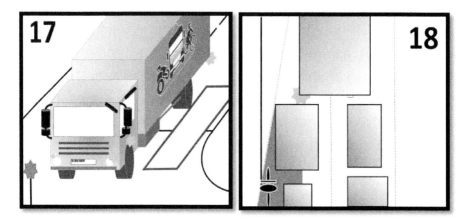

I cannot see you even though I want to. Also, imagine if you are approaching that traffic from behind as you can filter through to the junction. The vehicle behind me may be quite large and might obscure *your* view of my HGV. The light turns green and you start to accelerate to go through the lights. The stopped traffic starts to move off but you are still unable to see the HGV in the road in front. Imagine how that might look to you **(19).**

You wouldn't be able to see the road in front of the Bus so you might make the assumption there is a space there **(20)**. Consequently you could be hidden from the HGV Driver's view by this queueing traffic (depending on the road layout or size of vehicles behind me). As you know, HGV Drivers will try to look in their left mirrors during parts of the turn but if your speed interacts with where they are not looking, coupled with the fact that you have been obscured from their view as you approached the HGV, there is a real chance you will ride, unseen, into my Cab Blind-spot as I make the turn.

The Blind Part of the Turn

Related to where the HGV Driver will look, there is one other important bit of information you must remember: During the turn there will be a crucial point at which the HGV Driver will not be looking in *any* mirrors. This is the result of how the HGV Driver looks around their surroundings in combination with when they start to turn their HGV, and continue the turn until around the obstacle.

When the HGV Driver actually starts to turn they must keep in mind the width of their vehicle. You already know that this is a consideration for bringing the rear around but during this manoeuvre it now becomes about the front too. Before the HGV rear moves around the obstacle the front-right corner of the HGV becomes the most at-risk of hitting someone/thing **(21)**. This could be any Pedestrians stood at a central crossing or it could be queuing traffic. In either case the HGV may have to get quite close to them to bring the rear wheels around the kerb on the left **(22)**.

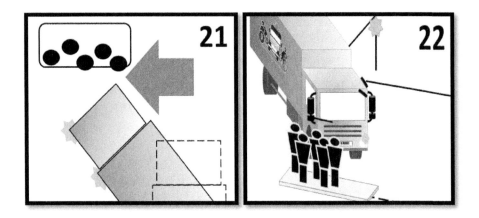

This is the crucial part of the turn for you as really it is when the HGV Driver needs to be looking in three separate directions all at the same time….and as you know the HGV Driver cannot do this. In theory, they must be looking diagonally left; they must be looking at their front-right corner and, because the rear wheels are close to Pedestrians… and because some road users choose to undertake HGVs, the HGV Driver must also be looking into their left mirrors **(23)**. This just cannot happen and for a few seconds, the HGV Driver cannot look at the left mirrors during a portion of the turn because the most at-risk chance of collision is at the front and right of their HGV.

 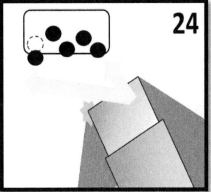

This will mean that the left and right mirrors will not be looked into for a number of seconds, and it may even be a few seconds longer if their attention is absorbed by somebody about to be endangered by that turning HGV **(24).** All of this will be happening *as the HGV is moving* so for a portion of the manoeuvre the HGV Driver will be moving left but CANNOT see what is on their left. As the HGV moves left, and *once* the HGV Driver knows the space they are moving into, and the front-right corner is safe, *then* they can look at their left mirrors **(25)**. This is to make sure that as they bring the HGV rear around the kerb they know the rear wheels are not endangering any Pedestrians. To do this they will need a clear picture of what is at the side of their HGV so will probably use the large, Main mirror that shows an undistorted view of the left side of their HGV.

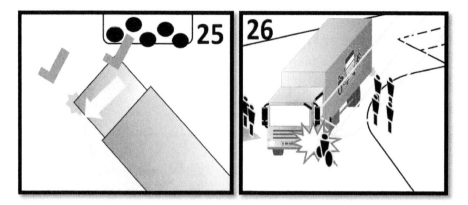

This will show a clear view of how close the rear wheels are to the kerb, but because the Main mirrors don't show straight down this is when you might be easily missed if your speed has already interacted with the HGV Driver's different glances, and if you have decided to undertake the HGV. The danger now is that you have been unseen as you have entered the Cab Blind-spot as the HGV Driver is *carrying out* their turn **(26)**.

This is also a danger for you if you decided to pass the HGV on its right side. I completely understand that having seen how you can be missed on the left it would make sense to think it safer to pass the HGV on its right side. Unfortunately, as the HGV Driver will be checking their left mirror prior to the turn then looking at their front, their front-right corner and then at their left mirror, because these pose the most chance of collision, the chances of them looking into their right mirrors are very small **(27)**.

The reason I mention this is because I know of an incident where a Cyclist was missed as they used the right side of the HGV. The

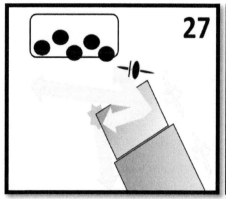 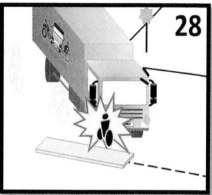

Cyclist's speed interacted with where the HGV Driver wasn't looking and their checks to the diagonal left, the front, the front-right corner and left mirror so did not see the Cyclist riding along the right side **(28)**. As the Cyclist reached the front of the HGV, which was already in the junction, they turned left, in front of the HGV and directly into the right-side Cab Blind-spot. Subsequently the HGV Driver unknowingly drove into the Cyclist and killed them. This is why the right side is not the safer option in a junction.

The Rear Wheels Take a Shorter Route

I have already spoken about the Required Space due to the length of the vehicle moving around corners: the HGV may often look like it is moving in a forwards direction when the intention of the HGV Driver is actually to turn. This is when the Front wheels are taking a wider, longer route than the rear wheels but this is needed to bring the rear wheels forwards to a certain point to safely make the turn **(29)**. This will always be needed to make sure the rear wheels don't drive over the kerb and endanger

Pedestrians. Where this becomes an issue for you, and how I want you to remember it, is the rear wheels will take a shorter route than the front wheels **(30).**

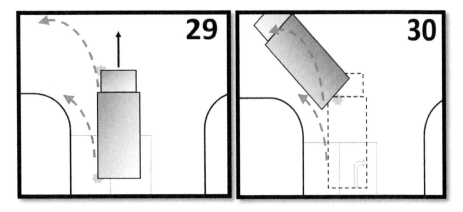

This is fundamental to any manoeuvring HGV and needs to be something you keep in mind if you have decided to undertake a HGV in a junction (but please don't). If you find yourself just in front of the rear wheels during a turn and keeping in mind some of the points from above, you may be caught out by how quickly the rear wheels start to turn and/or be missed by the HGV Driver.

Rear Wheels Take a Shorter Route & Articulated HGVs

The shorter route of the rear wheels is more prevalent on Articulated HGVs. Articulated HGVs are much longer than the Rigid bodied HGVs I have used in the book so far. As a result of their length the HGV Driver needs a lot more space to carry out their manoeuvres in certain junctions. In some junctions the HGV Driver may have decided to position themselves well over to the right of two lanes to make sure there is enough space to bring around the rear of the HGV when turning left. This creates the ultimate Illusion of Space as the HGV may not be able to fill the two lanes so leaves the entire inside lane open **(31)**. Even when the HGVs left indicator is on I regularly see all types of road-user enter this 'space'.

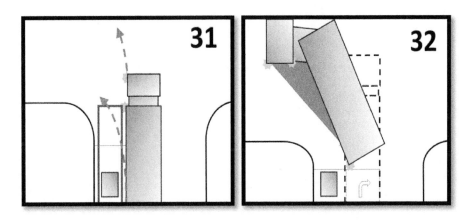

The danger to anyone entering that space is as soon as the HGV Driver is in the tight phase of the turn, and having to take into consideration everything I have mentioned above, their left mirrors may become completely useless as the trailer creates a Blind-spot, but, at the same time the length of the trailer suddenly closes the 'Illusion of Space' across the left hand lane **(32)**. Another attention-absorbing danger related to Articulated HGVs is that they are articulated. Due to the Cab turning independently from the trailer not only does the HGV Driver have a front, a front-right corner and left side to think about but they also now have the front-right and rear corners of the trailer to think about too **(33)**. This almost becomes a secondary vehicle that the HGV Driver must look at in their various mirrors to make sure it does not hit anything. As trailers are normally a lot higher than the Cab too the HGV Driver must now also keep in mind about how the height of that trailer might collide with street furniture such as road signs or even street lights **(34)**. This will mean another few seconds that the HGV Driver cannot look for you on their left or right. This is another reason not to pass on the left, or the right side of an Articulated HGV in a junction.

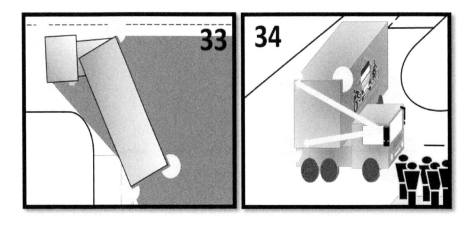

There is one more concern I would like you to think about related to Articulated HGVs. This may not be at the forefront of Cyclists' minds but I have seen this happen so it is worth mentioning here. This is what I saw:

I was positioned behind an Articulated HGV that was turning right. It was a small junction. They had used their size to fill both lanes of the junction to make sure there was enough space to bring around the rear wheels safely. As a result there was an Illusion of Space on the left side of that HGV. A Cyclist rode along the left side of me but because the lights had turned Green seconds earlier the Articulated HGV had already started to move forwards and turn right **(35).** Because the junction was small the rear wheels of the Articulated HGV only moved a few meters and then actually pivoted on the spot rather than move forwards. In turn, the back of the trailer actually span out wide to the left **(36).**

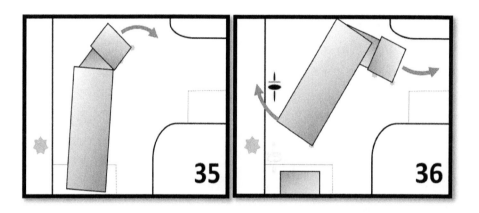

This could cause a danger to you if you decided to pass on the left as your route could be blocked by the sudden obstruction but, what I saw was the Cyclist safely pass in front of the spinning rear trailer but they were then 'chased' by the moving trailer which was only centimeters from the rear tyre of the Cyclist. As there is no engine noise at the rear of the HGV this was an approaching, silent danger that the Cyclist knew nothing about!

A little Summary

Phew! There's the manoeuvring section done. I know this chapter may have been a bit heavy in places but by sticking with it you truly are now becoming HGV Aware. I know there are lots of 'mights' and 'maybes' and the examples I have given you are really dependent at what point you interact with the HGV during a manoeuvre. This section was not to make excuses for HGV Drivers but to show you that there is more to it than just turning a wheel and 'not looking'. The road is a fluid, ever-changing environment so I really hope you can see what I have tried to do here. As you can see a HGV Driver cannot just turn the wheel and hope for the best as they have so many issues to take into consideration. I have shown you what I think is important information to help you while riding on our roads with HGVs. Please try and keep in mind what is here. Again, I completely understand that it is easy for me to say these things but I want to give you information that will help you stay safe.

Other Situational Examples

You now know what considerations the HGV Driver will be taking into account when they carry out a manoeuvre. With that fresh in your head I want to discuss some situational examples in which you may find yourself. These are based on incidents from the media, my own experiences and near-misses. At the end of this section I will also discuss the closest time I have come to being involved in a collision with a Cyclist...and the heart-stopping feeling that came from it.

Traffic Lights

I do want to discuss traffic lights. I know that other Countries are trialing schemes to allow Cyclists to go through Red lights but at this time, in the UK, it is against the law to go through a Red traffic light. The majority of Cyclists do stop at red lights. I see it every day at junctions in London and elsewhere and, yes, some Cyclists go through them *but* so do other road-users. Where this differs slightly is those Cyclists that decide to move through a Red light tend to do it whenever they *reach* a Red light, where as other road-users tend to go through just after they have changed to red...not always but that is what you normally see. I know that this is typically an educated decision by Cyclists because they can see that the road or Pedestrian crossing is clear. I know that it is tempting as when you cycle everyone wants

to maintain momentum but it is illegal, and if a Police Officer sees you do it you may be in line for a fine.

Another reason I imagine Cyclists tend to go through Red lights is because they use the same route and so get used to how the traffic flows at certain junctions. I understand that car traffic using the junction may never even encroach on your part of the road normally but please don't go through them. I want to give you an example that I have experienced on more than one occasion that I hope it will show you why you can't always go through them just because you think you know the flow of traffic.

My Experience

I have been pulling out of a side road or service road and wanting to turn right. It is a traffic-light controlled junction so I have right of way. The light turns Green, I do my mirror checks and I pull forward **(1)**. As I move forwards I can see the stopped traffic

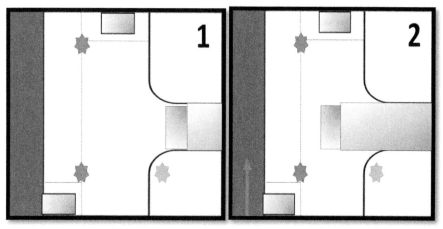

to my left and right, though I always make sure they have actually stopped before I commit to the manoeuvre. At this point a Cyclist, under the control of a red light, was riding along the bus lane **(2).**

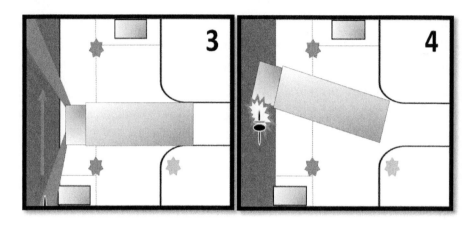

As I enter the junction my view is obscured by the queuing traffic to my left and then my vision is obscured by my left-side Mirror 'Beam' Blind-spot **(3).** I am also having to look to the right as I need to make sure the space I am about to occupy remains empty. I am looking out for Pedestrians who are still crossing the road and I am also looking into my right-hand side mirrors to make sure no Cyclists are moving up what will be the inside of the turn. I could not see the Cyclist riding along the Bus lane or when they came past the traffic due to my Mirror Blind-spot. They were then still missed because I needed to look right. By chance I quickly looked left to make sure no-one was moving up my left side and that is when I saw the Cyclist. We both slammed on our brakes and they just made contact with the front left of my Cab **(4)**.

The Cyclist had continued through their Red light because, I would imagine, there is a Bus lane either side of the junction and they thought it would be safe for them to continue straight through. It wasn't safe as my HGV needs to use all the space necessary to make sure the rear of my vehicle does not collide with the bollard or Pedestrian Island in the centre of the road. This has happened to me a number of times now. Some Cyclists have managed to get past me, just. Others have braked hard and stopped in time, and only one has gently hit me but luckily at a slow speed.

This is why I would ask you to not move through red lights. Yes it is illegal but I am not a Police Officer so can't tell you not to do it. I just want you to realise that the road may not always be clear, even if most days it might be.

HGVs Turning *Into* Your Road

For the majority of this book I have spoken about if you are on the road *with* a HGV and you have the choice to make the decision of how to interact with that HGV. I know that this is not always the case and I want to discuss one situation when you may be missed. I have already discussed Mirror Blind-spots and how the solidness of the mirror body can block the HGV Driver's vision, but I want to talk about if you see a HGV turning into your road as you are approaching the junction. You know what the HGV Driver should consider when turning left but one of the issues with turning left is the body of the left-side mirror obscuring the HGV

Driver's vision of the road they are entering. Let us say it is a smaller side road or the HGV is particularly long, the HGV Driver may have to use all of the width of the road they are entering to make sure the rear wheels of the HGV come around the kerb corner safely **(1,2)**.

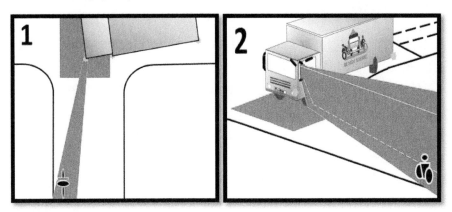

Yes, the HGV Driver should look around their mirror and check but please just be aware of this. As you are a small road user you can become hidden behind this mirror and as the HGV Driver checks their close surroundings they may miss you if your speed interacts with where they do not look **(3,4).**

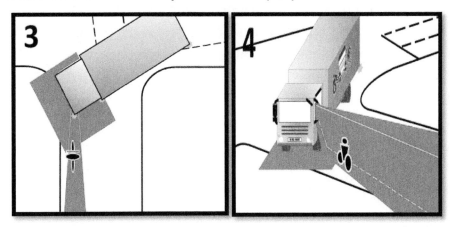

Again, I know it is easy to say but this book is about giving you information to help keep *you* safer so keep it in mind if you see a HGV turning towards you.

Reversing HGVs.

Quite regularly I have seen and experienced for myself Cyclists, Pedestrians and even car drivers continue past the rear of my HGV as I am reversing into a side/service road. Reversing is often done because there may be no way to turn around once in the side road. As a result the decision to reverse in would be taken because once the delivery has taken place it is safer to drive out forwards, onto a busy, main road rather than drive in and later attempt to reverse *out* onto a busy main road. I suppose I am making the assumption that others would see a reversing HGV as a potential danger to them, so they would want to allow the HGV to manoeuvre. Unfortunately I know this isn't the reality so I will explain why it is a potential danger to you.

As you already know the HGV Driver can only look in one direction at a time. Again, this is another example of the 1 o'clock, 9 o'clock hand exercise you did earlier in the book. As the HGV Driver will need a clear, undistorted view of the sides of their HGV they will tend to use the larger, Main mirrors on either side of the HGV **(1).** As you know these mirrors only show a very narrow view of the surrounding area and only one mirror can be seen at a time, so the HGV Driver is limited in what they can see especially if

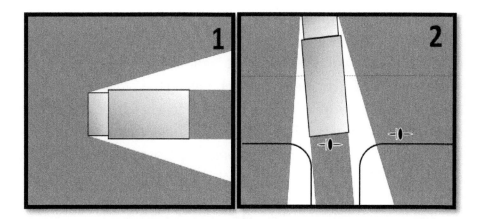

someone is approaching from the sides of their HGV **(2)**. If I were about to reverse my HGV into a side road I would slow down and put my hazard lights on, but try not to come to a complete stop as this may confuse other road users into thinking I am parking. If I do need to stop I will always try and park across my lane so others cannot get around me...as I will need to make sure the road is safe when I manoeuvre the HGV for the reverse **(3)**. If you do see a HGV put its hazard lights on there is a chance they will be positioning themselves for a reverse manoeuvre.

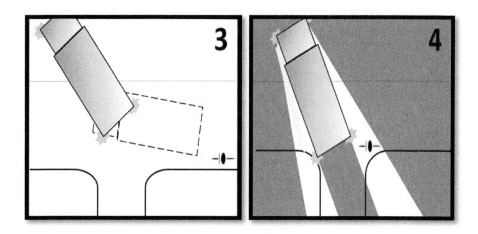

Keep in mind the space the HGV Driver is reversing into may be quite tight or there may be an obstacle particularly close to one side. So even if you do happen to stop inside *one* of the mirror views the HGV Driver may actually be using the *other* mirror more because that side of the HGV is closer to an obstacle that has more chance of a collision **(4)**. Consequently this may absorb more of the HGV Driver's attention therefore missing you. Of course the HGV Driver will try to look around as much as possible

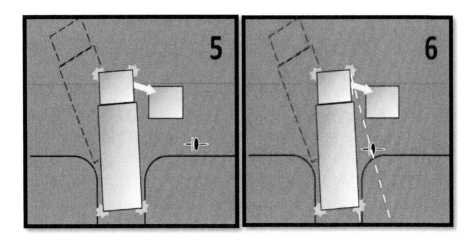

but during a reversing manoeuvre the biggest chance of hitting something will be at the rear and the sides of the HGV so that is where most of their attention will be. Also, during the manoeuvre and at different times, the HGV Driver must make sure the front side of the HGV Cab is not about to collide with another road user as it is straightened up. This will mean that the left or right mirrors cannot be seen as they look through their window **(5)**. This is another example of how you may be missed by the HGV Driver even though you may be inside what you know to be the narrow views of the Main mirrors **(6)**.

There may also be what is called a 'shunt'. This will happen if the HGV Driver is unable to get into the space on a first attempt due to the size of their HGV, the size of the space...or they may not have lots of experience yet. The shunt will be more common with an Articulated HGV as the HGV Driver will not always be able to see both sides of their vehicle and trailer but it can happen on a Rigid body HGV too. This is worth knowing as it will look like the reverse is finished (even though the HGV may look at a strange angle) but the HGV Driver is changing gear, then checking their surroundings to then pull forward, get a better angle and reverse again. The reason I mention this is because you may be cycling along the road and meet the HGV at this precise moment. You may have decided to move across the front of the HGV, because you think the HGV will continue to move backwards or because you think the manoeuvre is finished, and might be in the Cab Blind-spot as the HGV Driver pulls forward. Equally, you may think about passing the rear because you think the manoeuvre has finished when in fact it hasn't. Again, yes, it is easy for me to say this but please keep all of this in mind if you see a HGV slow for no reason with its hazard lights on. It may suddenly turn across the road or it may 'shunt' because the HGV Driver has not finished a reverse.

Roundabouts

I know I have gone into some detail of various HGV manoeuvring situations and your new knowledge will help you understand some of the issues HGV Drivers have with roundabouts, but cycling deaths have occurred at roundabouts and that is why I want to specifically discuss them here. The Cyclist I saw killed was at a roundabout too so this section is of particular significance to me.

Roundabouts are a bit of a nightmare for HGV Drivers in relation to keeping Cyclists safe. In fact any larger vehicle will find roundabouts more dangerous to manoeuvre around in the urban environment. This is due to the amount of activity on roundabouts, the different types of manoeuvres required and the Blind-spots that are produced by those increased manoeuvres.
Even looking at the worn away verges on some large roundabouts on UK *motorway* junctions you can see roundabouts are not always designed to accommodate a turning HGV so imagine how the HGV Driver must feel when faced with a small city roundabout really only designed for cars.

Similar to the Left Turn mentioned previously I want to talk through how the HGV will move around the Roundabout, where the HGV Driver will probably be looking, and how that will affect your safety. I am going to discuss a HGV that is turning right. This is because a HGV moving around a roundabout to the right actually contains a number of different manoeuvres to make sure the rear is brought around safely at each point. Again, I am not going to position you as the road is a very fluid environment. I want you to think about how the HGV Driver's different manoeuvres and glances will affect you depending on when you interact with the HGV. So here goes.

Positioning

Often roundabouts within the urban environment are not built for a turning HGV. The lanes are too narrow and this is where the HGV Driver's training will come into effect even more. The HGV Driver must make sure they have the space to bring round the rear of their vehicle. So like the Left Turn the HGV Driver may have to position themselves over both lanes to make sure a) they have the Required Space to get the rear of the HGV around

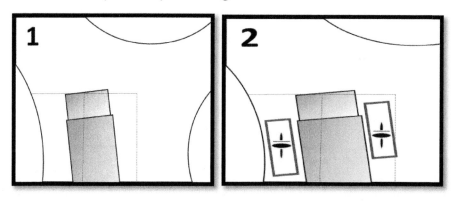

safely, and b) use their Defensive Driving techniques to reduce the chance of other road users from becoming endangered during the manoeuvre (even on single-laned approaches to roundabouts the HGV Driver may position themselves as far right as they can within their lane (1)). Unfortunately, like the Left Turn, this creates the Illusion of Space on the left side of the HGV and can also create it on the right side too. While this may stop car drivers from entering that 'space' it does not stop you from having the ability to enter it on your bicycle (2). As you know though, this space will disappear as soon as the HGV starts to turn.

Joining the Roundabout.

Without meaning to state the obvious the first thing you must remember about roundabouts is that the traffic on them comes from the right, so the HGV Driver will be looking towards the right **(3)**. The reason I say this is as a small, more agile road-user this is where you are going to get lost on the left as the HGV Driver looks for that space in the traffic. That is the direction the HGV Driver will be looking for the *majority* of the time while waiting to join the roundabout, just like you look to the right as well. The HGV Driver may well look occasionally into their left side mirrors to check for you but what if you aren't in that mirror as they check? For that split second the HGV Driver thinks it is clear and then looks back to the right.

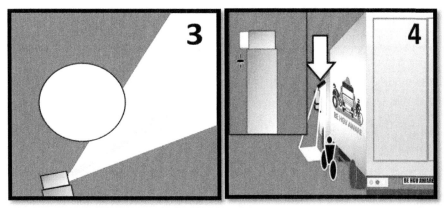

Once there is space to join the roundabout the HGV Driver should check the left-side mirror as they pull out but, again, what if they look in their close proximity mirror first and you're not in that mirror? **(4)**

…or, what if you have already moved down the side of the HGV and the HGV Driver looks into their wide-angle mirror first and misses you because you are in the Cab Blind-spot and thinks it is clear? **(5)**. What if the HGV Driver doesn't actually check their left mirror? This may be the reality as they look for a gap in very busy traffic to fit into on the roundabout? **(6)**.

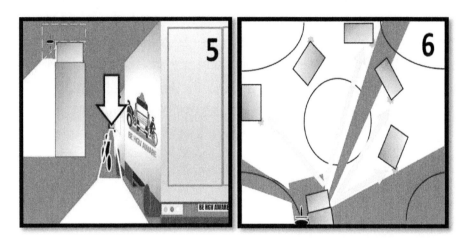

This may even include looking for turning indicators on any vehicle including those straight across or even on the left side of the roundabout to see what is joining. This will allow the HGV Driver to judge when to pull out. All of this is important to you because it means the HGV Driver is not looking into their left mirrors for a significant amount of time. Again I know you may not like it and it isn't perfect but that may be the reality when a HGV Driver is waiting to join a roundabout.

Manoeuvring on the Roundabout

On entering a roundabout the HGV Driver will move forwards and the first part of their manoeuvre will be a Left turn. You already know what is involved in a Left turn, and the many considerations the HGV Driver has as I have discussed it above but the main considerations when turning on a roundabout are a) trying to make sure their surroundings are clear b) making sure the front of the HGV does not hit anyone already on the roundabout c) bringing the rear of the HGV around the kerb safely and d) take into consideration the size of the HGV in relation to the roundabout and assessing how wide each part of the manoeuvre will have to be.

As in image 2 the Illusion of Space is already being created on both sides when the HGV is positioned to *join* the roundabout. As the HGV Driver moves forwards the Illusion of Space is *still* in existence on both sides. At this point, the HGV Driver will need to be looking into their left side mirrors (to check for you) but also at their front, right corner as this also has a high chance of collision with road-users already on the roundabout. As you know the HGV Driver cannot look in both places at the same time so the HGV Driver will have to alternate between the two areas…each of which are on opposite sides. The front, right corner may take priority for a few seconds as they don't want to collide with anyone already on the roundabout **(7)**. If you have chosen to move along the left side of the HGV then you may be missed at that point.

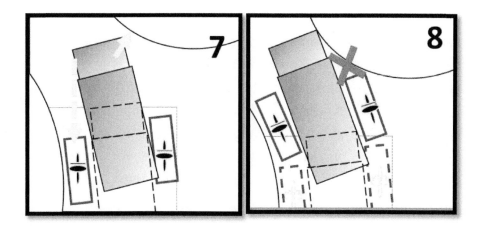

As the HGV continues to move forwards and the Cab reaches the centre of the roundabout, and if you are moving along the right side because you know the left side to be dangerous, your 'space' to move is now removed until the full length of the HGV has passed that point **(8)**. While the HGV is not going to collide with you if you are near the rear of the HGV this may leave you now sitting in the centre of the roundabout waiting for the HGV to pass you, and directly in the path of oncoming traffic **(8)**. Equally though, let's say the HGV Driver has been looking into their left mirrors more…because the roundabout is quite empty, they may not have seen you cycling along their right side. You may be inside the right-side, Cab Blind-spot as the HGV is driven forwards and towards the centre of the roundabout. This is where it could collide with you!

Once the HGV Driver manoeuvres to this point they will then look towards their left (to make sure the space they are about to occupy remains safe, just like the Left turn) and then start to turn the HGV to the left while looking into their left side mirrors to make sure the rear wheels on the left do not hit the left-side kerb. This is when the Illusion of Space on the left now starts to disappear as the rear wheels take a shorter route than the front wheels did. If you have ridden along the left side at this point (due to the Illusion of Space), and depending on where you have positioned yourself, the HGV Driver may miss you as your movement interacts with whichever mirror the HGV Driver isn't looking into.

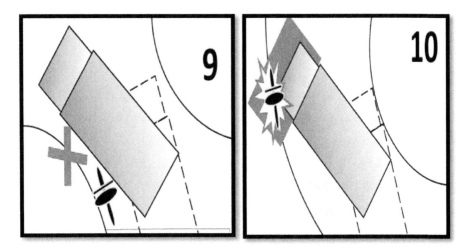

(9). This is really important for you because not only is the HGV moving left, and closing the 'Illusion of Space' on the left of the HGV but the HGV Driver must also then position themselves for the *next* part of the roundabout, which will be a Right turn.

This will mean there is a chance that the HGV Driver will have to manoeuvre the front Left of the HGV even wider to the left to make sure the *right-side rear* wheels are then in a position to be brought around the centre of the roundabout safely. You may use the roundabout every day, there may always be a safe route around the edge of that roundabout *with cars* but this could be very different with a HGV. It may mean the HGV Driver has to bring the left side of the HGV really close to the left-side kerb and your normal, safe route will disappear **(10).** If you have managed to get past the HGV safely on the left side, yet unseen by the HGV Driver, you may be hit from the side as the Cab Blind-spot envelops you.

At this point it means the HGV Driver will be looking diagonally left at the front of the HGV because they need to judge how close the front, left corner of the Cab is to the left-side kerb **(11).** This will mean that the right-side mirrors cannot be seen (because the HGV Driver is looking left) but because the HGV Driver is creating

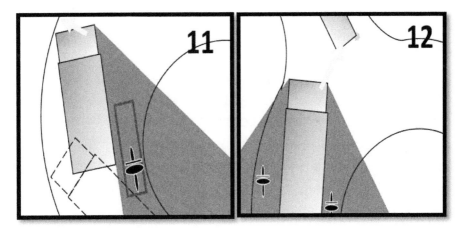

room for themselves by moving as far to the left as they can (to safely bring around the rear right-side of the HGV) the next Illusion of Space is now being created on the right-side of the HGV. Consequently you may see the "space" appear and think it is safe to enter as the rear wheels seem to be moving away from the centre of the roundabout **(11).** There is space right then but, as you know, that space will disappear without you knowing when.

The HGV Driver may then need to be looking at vehicles joining the roundabout from the first exit/entrance junction **(12)**. We all know HGVs can be slow and especially during a manoeuvre; as a result other road users see this slowness as a chance to ignore the 'give way to vehicles coming from the right' rule to get in front of HGVs. Unfortunately, this is another example of the attention-absorbing nature of the road meaning that you may not be seen because the HGV Driver has to look that little bit longer towards the area in front of their vehicle. Depending on how many exit/entrance junctions there are will mean just how much the HGV Driver will need to look at traffic joining the road, and if they are looking at the front then they are not looking into their right or left mirrors **(12)**.

Once the HGV Driver sees it is safe to move past the exit/entrance junction and continue around the roundabout, (because no one is entering the roundabout) they will continue with their manoeuvre and move the HGV to the right. As the rear wheels are again taking a shorter route than the front wheels, it will also mean the 'Illusion of Space' that existed on the right of the HGV (in image 11) is now being closed **(13)**. You could be missed but, like in the Left Turn, the HGV Driver will check their right-side mirrors once they know the front of their vehicle is safe. This is to make sure their rear wheels on the right do not hit the roundabout's centre kerb. This will mean that the left side of the HGV cannot now be seen **(13)**.

Once the HGV Driver has brought the right-side, rear wheels around the centre kerb safely they must then position themselves for another Left turn *into* their exit junction **(14)**. The HGV Driver will manoeuvre the Cab straight and, like the Left turn, this may look like the HGV isn't going to turn at all. This is to make sure

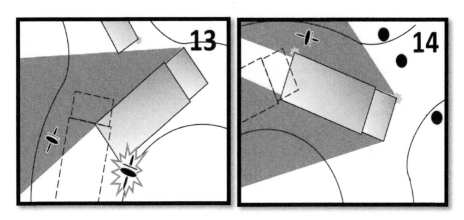

there is enough space to bring the left-side, rear wheels around safely without hitting the kerb that may have Pedestrians crossing or waiting to cross. Again, this may mean the HGV Driver's attention is absorbed and they may not see you if you are close to the HGV as neither the left and right mirrors can be seen at this moment **(14)**. Just like the Left turn this will mean all of the considerations of the HGV Driver coming back into play. The most important for you being a) that there will be a point of the turn that neither side of the HGV can be seen because the HGV Driver will be looking into the space they are *going* to occupy **(15)**, and b) the 'Illusion of Space' appearing on the left and then closing as the left-side rear wheels are brought around the exit kerb **(16)**.

Summary

I know I have mentioned this a few times now but the rear wheels will always take a shorter route than the front wheels due to the length of the HGV, and this is fundamental to understanding why the HGV will manoeuvre the way it does on a roundabout. The HGV Driver needs to create the Required Space to bring the HGV

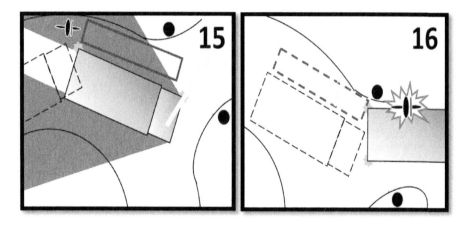

into the roundabout, *around* the roundabout, and then create space to *exit* the roundabout without hitting anyone or anything...and at the same time try to drive defensively as much as possible to stop other road users being endangered by their HGV and to look out for smaller road-users such as Cyclists.

Because all of this is going on the HGV Driver's visual limitations on roundabouts are a combination of the Physical Obstructions caused by the design of the Cab and the Observational Blind-spots. Consequently the HGV Driver has multiple, continually changing 'at risk' points. This is why, if it is your decision, it is very important that you never attempt to pass a HGV while they are on a roundabout as you will never know where the HGV Driver is looking or how the HGV Driver has assessed how they will carry out their manoeuvre. This is another reason why it is safer to stay behind the HGV and take the lane…if possible.

With regard to roundabouts I suppose I am a bit more influenced by my experience. I want you to know what may be going on within the HGV Cab as I have seen the consequences of what goes wrong when a HGV Driver misses a Cyclist.

I want to try and explain what happened on that day as I believe it is worth learning from the incident. On that day the HGV Driver was turning left and was joining a busy, London roundabout.

What I Saw on That Day…

Image 1

The HGV Driver will have been looking towards the right for a gap on the busy roundabout, so may not have been looking into their left mirrors. There is also a chance that the Cyclist could have been obscured by the queuing traffic behind the HGV...though the chances are probably greater that the HGV Driver wasn't looking left.

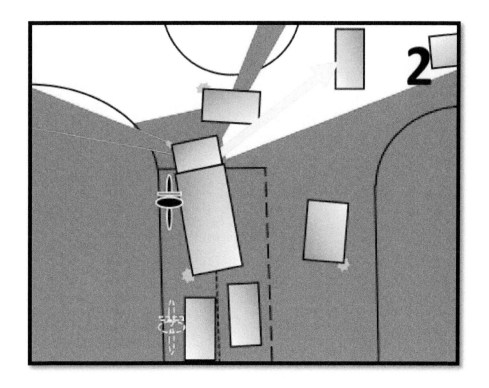

Image 2

The Cyclist had filtered along the left of the queuing traffic but then undertook along the inside (Blindside) of the moving HGV.

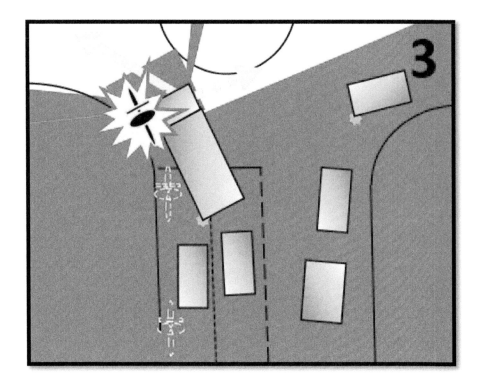

Image 3

As the HGV Driver saw a gap they probably started to pull forward as they were turning their head (only they will know if they looked in any of their left side mirrors).

At the same time the Cyclist entered the Cab Blind-spot and the HGV Driver hit the Cyclist with the corner of the Cab.

Image 4

Only after most of the HGV had turned into the corner did the HGV Driver then check their left-side mirror to make sure the rear wheels did not hit the kerb. This may have been a result of checking the space they were going to occupy remained safe, and checking the front, right corner of their HGV Cab (the 'Blind' part of the turn I spoke about). Once the front was safe the HGV Driver then probably checked their left side mirrors and this is when I imagine they saw something behind their rear wheels in the road. The reason I think this is because the HGV Driver only stopped once the full length of the HGV was past the point of collision.

You may ask 'why didn't the HGV Driver feel anything?' HGVs are big, solid pieces of engineering with tough, reinforced tyres and suspension that is not designed so much for comfort but to cushion the weight of the HGV (with a full load) from the surface of the road. This can make the ride within a HGV quite bumpy so air-cushioned seats have been fitted to help alleviate the sometimes stiffness of the ride. Unfortunately driving over a person on a bicycle would not have felt much different to driving over a pothole or sunken drain cover…if they felt anything at all.

If I am being honest I do believe that the HGV Driver could have done more to look on their left but I also believe that the Cyclist should never have put themselves in that position. Did the HGV Driver look into one of their left mirrors and miss the Cyclist because of the size of the Cab or the mirror they chose to look into? I just don't know. It was a Construction/Tipper-type HGV with a really high Cab and this type of HGV will have enormous Blind-spots surrounding the Cab, but whatever did happen within that Cab led to a Cyclist being missed and being killed…which should never have happened.

The unimaginably violent and brutal way in which the Cyclist was killed will stay with me forever but it will be nothing when compared to the loss and pain of the victims' family…or the grief and guilt of the HGV Driver involved. It was horrible on so many levels. The instant and eternal thoughts of those affected by one incident is something that has stayed with me since that day. Not to forget the feelings of those affected by that event, because you can't, but on a personal note that was a turning point for me. I always thought of myself as a conscientious HGV Driver, and I have always driven around with the question 'what if' in my head. *What if* they stop? Where do I go? *What if* someone comes out of that side road now? What do I do? I constantly have the 'what if' in my head, but since that day I have always taken that extra glance, that extra check in another mirror just to make sure that never happens to me. It was also the motivation for 'Be HGV Aware' so, I hope, one small positive has come from it as I try to help other vulnerable road users stay safer.

My Closest Experience...

With each chapter fresh in your mind, this is where I would like to tell you about a personal experience I once had. It is not the incident in which I saw a Cyclist killed, as I was not the HGV Driver involved but it is the one time I know that a Cyclist escaped without injury or possible death only by luck. This experience is the closest encounter I have ever had of nearly being involved in a serious incident with a Cyclist.

I was in London. I was driving along Chelsea Embankment with the Thames River to my left. Chelsea Embankment is a very wide road that in places you could comfortably get two vehicles side-by-side or a segregated cycle-way but at that time, for some reason, remained a very wide, single-lane road.

This changes when you approach a traffic-light controlled junction as there are roads that cross the river. At these junctions two lanes are marked on the road but they are very narrow and are just big enough for two cars to get through side-by-side. They are no way big enough for a HGV to negotiate the junction without using two lanes **(1)**. Equally, on the other side of that particular junction there is a left bend so I knew I had to create the 'Required Space' to bring around my left-side rear wheels without hitting the kerb stone. On approaching the junction the Red lights were causing congestion and two lanes were full of traffic. I was positioned in the left lane and was unable to move into the right lane at that time **(2)**.

I had looked into my left Main mirror and I had seen a Cyclist at least 150m behind me; they were filtering between the left side of the traffic and the kerb **(3)**. I was keeping an eye on the Cyclist and I was also then looking at the traffic lights. I had my right indicator on and as we started to move forwards on the Green light. I was also watching my right side to try and move over slightly for my 'Required Space' **(4)**. Unfortunately no-one was letting me into the right lane but I wanted to make sure I had enough room to bring around the rear of my HGV as I drove through the junction, and as the junction narrowed.

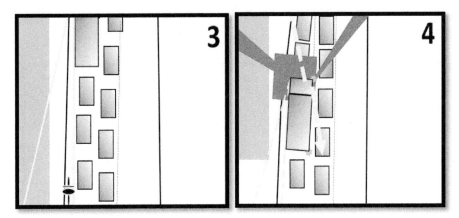

I was getting closer to the traffic light junction and by this point the road had narrowed so much that there was no room between me and the left side kerb, effectively blocking the path of the Cyclist **(5)**.

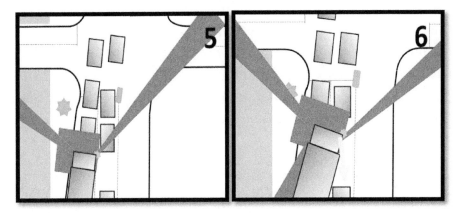

As the traffic slowly moved further forwards I saw a space appear on my right **(6)**.

The car driver on my right was looking down into their lap...I imagine at a mobile-phone but it was the space I needed. I moved my HGV into this space but had to make quite a deliberate move to the right. I then looked into my left mirror but the view of the road was now a Blind-spot due to the angle of my HGV **(6)**. I looked back to my right to check the space I was moving into.

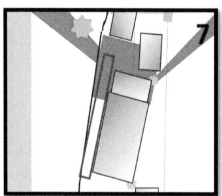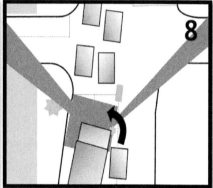

As I was straightening up for the junction, and trying to fill both lanes for my 'Required Space', I created the Illusion of Space on my left **(7)**. At the same time as this, and when the HGV was not quite filling both lanes, the car driver who had been looking down into their lap decided that they did not want to be behind my HGV so aggressively accelerated and overtook me in a gap that was close to disappearing. The car was obviously a lot quicker than me but only managed to overtake me by moving into the on-coming traffic lane **(8)**.

Luckily I heard the engine and saw what they were doing. The car driver just managed to get through the gap between me and the island but only because I reacted quickly and impulsively steered

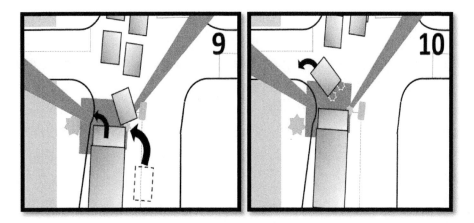

my HGV away from the car towards the left. I did not have time to look left as it was an instant reaction to stopping an incident occurring. As I steered the HGV to the left, the front left corner of the HGV would have moved towards the kerb and significantly closed the Illusion of Space **(9)**. To make things worse, rather than just carry on straight, the car driver, having accelerated hard past my HGV Cab, then slammed on their brakes because they wanted to turn left onto the bridge!. I was just starting to turn my head to look into my left mirrors but saw the cars brake lights come on. I reacted to the brake lights by braking too but not coming to a complete stop. This now meant I still hadn't checked my left mirrors for a few seconds due to the behaviour of the car driver but my front, left Cab corner was now almost touching the kerb **(10)**.

I knew the Cyclist would be very near and quickly looked into my Main mirror first **(11)**. I thought…hoped…they may have stayed to the rear of me seeing that the road narrowed at the junction. I didn't see them in the Main mirror so quickly looked into my Wide-angle mirror **(12)**. They weren't there either?!...

It is amazing how many thoughts fly through your head in just a matter of milliseconds but I was panicking.

Where were they? Were they still behind me? Had I hit them as I turned away from the car? I hadn't heard anything but then again would I hear anything?? I'm far too close to the kerb for them to be next to me, surely? I was about to look into my Close-proximity mirror and suddenly, I saw them ride out of my Cab Blind-spot...with what must have been millimeters between their rear wheel and my HGV front bumper!

I S**T MYSELF! ...And stamped on my brake pedal!

They didn't look particularly happy either. They were bright red with a mixture of sheer panic and anger on their face. If I hadn't been sure about this anger I was made aware of it because of the collection of hand gestures they then gave me. I completely understood the reaction as I was thinking the same too. Why were

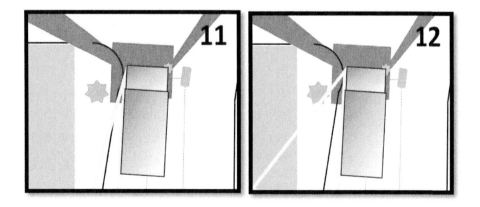

they there in the first place?! I don't mean on the road. I mean right next to me in the junction?!

Yes, I knew the Cyclist was on the road, but from about image **6** I didn't know where. My view on the left had been obscured by the angle of my HGV, and my attention had been absorbed by the behaviour of someone else, *but* they also chose to ride, at speed, 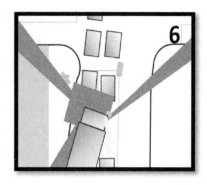 through a junction, while undertaking a HGV and on a narrowing lane.

I do not know if there is a chance I would have seen them but because of their speed, the behavior of others, the grey (tarmac-coloured) jogging bottoms, and the dark green jumper they were wearing while riding along a shadow-covered, tree-lined road, I did not see them. Would Hi-Vis 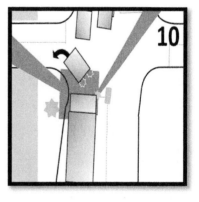 have helped here? I don't know...probably not as the road was over shadowed by the trees. Would a flashing light have helped here? It may have.

I might have picked it up in the Wide-angle mirror and in my left-side peripheral vision as I started to look left (but then reacted to the brake lights in image 10) but who knows. All I know is that they were very lucky to have walked away from that.

I safely overtook them a few hundred meters later. I pulled over, got out and gestured for them to stop. I wanted to talk to face-to-face and ask if they were alright but I also wanted to try and explain why what they had done was so dangerous. I spoke about how Blind-spots 'work' and where I was having to look. I explained that I can't look in my left mirror *all* of the time, just like they wouldn't ride their bike looking over their left shoulder *all* the time. I asked why they were right next to me and their reply was "well, you're the professional Driver. You should be looking out for me". I was quite surprised by that response. I think I replied something like 'that's true but that doesn't mean you should behave like an amateur'. Their response was 'well, I don't think I did anything wrong and that was your fault'. I understood that they were angry but I was actually quite saddened by this opinion. They took no responsibility for any of their actions and they had surrendered their safety to me.

It is a coming together of everything I have mentioned in this book. I had Physical Blind-spots caused by the Cab design and the trailer, and I had Observational Blind-spots caused by where I was looking. This meant other areas couldn't be looked into: if I can't see you, I can't keep you safe. The road layout affected the manoeuvre and my ability to see; attention-absorbing behavior of other road-users then affected my ability to see; the Cyclist moved faster than the surrounding traffic in the junction which meant I then had less time to see them; the filtering versus undertaking paradox was certainly present: I saw it as undertaking a HGV in a junction. They saw it as filtering; the Cyclist surrendered their personal safety; they were not aware of how they might blend into the scenery or shadows due to their clothing but the most important point is that the Cyclist made the assumption they had been seen by me.

I have been criticised for using words like 'assumed' and 'assumption' but that is the one thing I hope I have shown you throughout this book: Never assume that you have been seen by the HGV Driver because nothing tells you that you have been seen. Please, because of what I have shown you and when interacting with HGVs, always ask yourself one question:

Have I Been Seen?

And the only answer you can have is

I Can't Know

The above question is one that I want you to remember when interacting with HGVs as I want it to remind you of this book. If it is your choice to decide how you interact then please, always ask yourself that question. Hopefully that will then dictate how you act.

Summary

I really hope you can see just how difficult it is for a HGV Driver to see Cyclists on their left *and* right during a turn. There are so many attention-absorbing factors affecting the HGV Driver, and places they know they must look, that they cannot see all of them. I know I must look in one direction but this means other directions will not be looked into during parts of the turn. I need to be looking out for hazards in front of me.

THE MIRRORS WILL NOT BE LOOKED INTO DURING PARTS OF THE TURN AS I NEED TO BE LOOKING OUT FOR HAZARDS IN FRONT OF ME.

They just can't be as this would not be safe for the road-users *in front* of the turning HGV or in the space the HGV is going to occupy.

The HGV Driver knows they must check their front but they also know they must be looking to see what is on their left-hand side, plus look to see what is on their right-hand side, plus look to see what is *in* their left-hand mirrors plus, look to see what is *in* their right-hand mirrors plus, look into their close-proximity mirror *and* their front-bumper mirror. As I have shown you with the 1 o'clock 9 o'clock exercise, there is no way the HGV Driver can look in all of these directions at the same time. It is just physically impossible to look in *all* of these directions *all* at the same time and this is where Cyclists may be missed and a collision may occur. If, on top of this, a Cyclist now decides to undertake the

HGV, moving at a speed faster than the traffic, and break the rules that the majority are working to, you can really see just how difficult it may be for the HGV Driver to have *time* to see that Cyclist.

Now you might say 'well, the HGV Driver should look into the mirror that corresponds to the most at-risk Blind-spot'. You are right but which one is that? Is it the one on the left, where Pedestrians and Cyclists have been missed and hit? Is it the one on the right, where Pedestrians and Cyclists have been missed and hit? Is it the space where the HGV is moving into, where Pedestrians and Cyclists have been missed and hit? You can see the problem the HGV Driver has. As a result the HGV Driver must make snap decisions as to where and when to look to make sure they are not going to hit someone/thing and equally, not have someone/thing hit them…and that is when a HGV Driver *is* doing everything they can to see their surroundings, so imagine what a HGV Driver doesn't see when they *aren't* doing everything they can to see their surroundings. Also, imagine if one of those variables mentioned above absorbs the attention of the HGV Driver a bit longer than you thought it might such as a car's brake lights coming on, or a Pedestrian running across the road, or another Cyclist riding up the other side of the HGV that you are on.

All of these factors will affect if you are seen so please keep this chapter in mind when cycling near HGVs.

PLEASE REMEMBER:

- DOES THE HGV DRIVER KNOW THE JUNCTION?

- THE NOISE OF THE AIR BRAKES IS YOUR WARNING THE HGV IS ABOUT TO MOVE.

- HOW THE ATTENTION-ABSORBING SURROUNDINGS MAY AFFECT THE HGV DRIVER'S GLANCES.

- THE RIGHT SIDE OF THE HGV IS NOT SAFER.

- THE HGV MAY LOOK LIKE IT IS GOING STRAIGHT AHEAD BUT THEN QUICKLY TURN.

- WHERE WILL THE HGV DRIVER LOOK DURING A TURN??

- HGV DRIVERS NEED TO BE LOOKING OUT FOR HAZARDS IN FRONT OF THEM TOO.

- THE CRUCIAL, 'BLIND POINT' DURING ANY TURN.

- THE REAR WHEELS TAKE A SHORTER ROUTE THAN THE FRONT WHEELS.

- ARE YOU ACTUALLY HIDDEN FROM VIEW?

- THE SAFEST PLACE TO BE IS AT THE REAR OF THE HGV.

- HAVE YOU BEEN SEEN? YOU CAN'T KNOW.

Left-hand drive/Foreign HGV's

Just before we move onto the last chapter I do want to mention something I would like you to think about. This book has discussed Right-hand drive HGVs so the Blind-spots discussed throughout are related to those types of HGV. At some point though you may encounter Left-hand drive/Foreign HGVs on UK roads.

I am not going to discuss this in detail but what I would like you to remember is, because the HGV Driver is sat on the *left* of their HGV, the Blind-spots have changed slightly. In fact they have reversed to what I have shown you in this book.

The Rear Blind-spot remains the same but the Mirrors, and especially the Cab Blind-spot switch sides and as this book is about giving you information to help you stay safer I want you to know this.

The Mirrors

As the HGV Driver is on the left the angle of the Blind-spot 'Beams' are slightly different. The Left-side Mirror is now the closest to the HGV Driver and the right-side Mirror furthest away. I would like you to remember that because those 'beams' are at slightly different angles and it may affect you if you see a Left-hand drive...

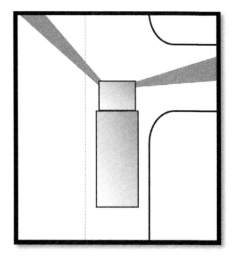

HGV approaching a junction (as discussed on page 55, 56).

The Cab

This is probably the most important Blind-spot change that I want you to know. Throughout this book I have really tried to get across just how dangerous the Cab Blind-spot can be. On a Left-hand drive HGV this Blind-spot now sits on the right of the HGV and is now dangerous during a *right turn,* especially if you happen to be on the right of that HGV. Please stay at the rear so you 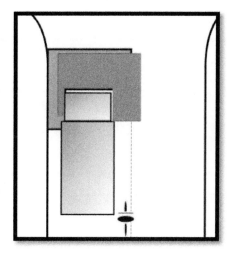 can be seen within the Mirrors. That is because the right side is now the **Blindside.**

Again, I know it is easy for me to say be careful of this. This is just an extra bit of information I want you to think about. I did not want to confuse you with Right-hand vs Left-hand drive HGVs throughout the book as I didn't think that would help you. What I have shown you in this book should be your main considerations when cycling on the roads but, please, keep in the back of your mind the chance that the HGV near you may be a Left-hand drive HGV. Consequently the HGV Drivers' Blind-spots are different.

If you have the time then please try and have a look at what type of number plate a HGV has. This is your biggest clue the HGV

Driver may be sat on the left, if approaching a HGV from behind. If it is similar to those shown here then there is an almost

guaranteed chance that the Blind-spots, and where the HGV Driver will be looking will be opposite to what I have shown you in this book.

.

Being Seen

Be Seen

There are things you can do to help HGV Drivers see you. The information I have given you so far means you know that not all mirrors can be looked into at the same time. As a result you know that it comes down to where the HGV Driver is looking in combination with your positioning that will determine when you are seen.

Positioning

Positioning is key. If it is your choice the best place to position yourself in relation to a HGV is at the rear and to the side **(1)**. This will mean the HGV Driver will see you when they look in their Main mirrors on the left or right depending on your intentions **(2)**. This is the safest place to be with a HGV in or near a junction, and the safest place to stay while a HGV carries out a manoeuvre.

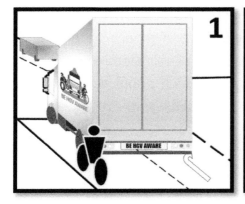 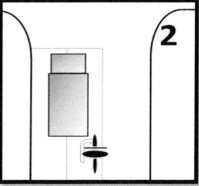

Unfortunately, this is where the reality of using the road takes over. You will not always be in perfect 'text book' conditions. You are in a fluid, ever-changing environment and may suddenly find yourself near a HGV or bus that you hadn't seen: it was blocked from view, it approached from a side road or it approached you from behind. That is the reality of the road and until segregated cycle-ways exist on our roads this is a reality that will exist for the foreseeable future, but please, if it is your choice, try and think about your positioning with regard to the Blind-spots and the observational limitations of the HGV Driver.

Training

On passing my car driving test I was once told 'You've learnt how to pass your test, now you learn how to drive'. This is where I am going to mention training. As a HGV Driver I have received training on how to pass my test and drive the HGV correctly, but that test is far more involved than a car test. I continued to have driver training with each company I worked for. Every 6 to 12 months I would be taken out by a Driver Trainer and they would assess my driving skills. This was useful as it stopped me picking up bad habits but it also made me think about how someone would see my driving behaviour. As a HGV agency Driver I was also regularly assessed when going to work for a new company. Again, this keeps in mind my driving behaviour and trying to remain as professional as possible.

The reason I mention this is that during my last 'Safe Urban Driving' course (HGV Drivers taken out on bicycles to experience cycling in the urban environment) our Cycling Instructor actually admitted that he had never had any road cycling training when he first started. He had a car license but cycled to work and was getting into altercations with other road users. Someone suggested to him that he take some lessons. He said he was a bit insulted by the suggestion but decided to take the advice. Consequently he said he gained a useful experience from the training and, as a result, he eventually quit his job and became a Cycling Instructor. I am telling you this because if you haven't had any training it might be useful to get some. This book is not official cycling training as I am not a Cycling Instructor...and I am not going to pretend it is, it is just extra, specific knowledge and one small aspect of road safety. I understand you may hold a car license but obviously cycling is different to driving a car and cycling training may make you aware of issues you had never thought of. If, on the other hand you don't hold a driving license then I would suggest some sort of cycling training, even if it's only to know what rules everyone else should be following when on the road. It will also help with how you position yourself. You may never have thought about your positioning before but it will make such a difference.

One thing you can do around HGVs is actually just slow down or more accurately, equal the speed of the traffic around you...but make sure you do this so the HGV Driver can see you (positioning). This is going to increase your chances of being seen as the HGV Driver looks around their vehicle. This may sound really simple but during a manoeuvre you now know there are so many places a HGV Driver must look. The HGV Driver needs your help and slowing down will help them see you.

If you slow down at the rear and to the side of a HGV then this will give the HGV Driver that bit more time to see you, particularly in junctions. I am not saying you have to slow down all the time near HGVs but it is a useful skill to adopt if approaching any HGV in a junction.

How You are Seen

I have said in the introduction that I hope that one day this book doesn't matter, and that is related to having designated cycling infrastructure, the majority embracing cycling or at least accepting that others want to cycle and that will mean more Cyclists on the road. Until that point though, today, next week, next month and next year it will mean that Cyclists and HGV Drivers will be on the same roads together. That is why, at the *moment*, it is still a good idea to think about your visibility to help HGV Drivers see you.

I like to use my former military training here as a way of getting across my point. During my Basic Training I was taught in the skills of Camouflage and Concealment: how to blend into my surroundings and make myself harder to see. I was taught about breaking up the recognisable head and shoulders Shape and Silhouette of the human form, as this is something that the human eye and brain will naturally look for. I was taught about removing

Shine, so light could not reflect off my skin or kit. I was taught about Shadows and how they could give away my positon but equally, how I could use them to hide. I was also taught about Sound, and how to secure noisy bits of equipment so as not to make noise while moving.

Shape, Silhouette, Shine, Shadow and Sound

Now you may think that a Soldier concealing themselves while thinking about the above has nothing to do with commuting by bicycle, but I would disagree. They have everything to do with cycling, just in their opposite capacity: you are not trying to conceal yourself but make yourself stand out.

I want you to think about the colours of the urban environment: grey concretes, dull red brick, black tarmac, dull red bus lanes, beige footpaths, grey shadows, glass reflections, greenery. Also, think about the colours of many of the vehicles you see on the road: greys, blues, whites, blacks, silvers, reds. Imagine how the urban environment looks when it is dirty, or it's overcast, or it's rainy…this is the UK. So if you were a Soldier trying to conceal yourself in this environment what colours would you wear? Greys, blacks, blues, beiges; a dark suit? Blue/black jeans? Khaki trousers or jacket, beige trousers? A white or red top? Obviously there are lots of other colours but these are colours that you generally see people wearing in the street, and these are also the colours that you will blend into when I look out of my windscreen or into the very flat, two dimensional world of my mirrors. You may think a white, red, yellow, bright blue top or rucksack will be bright enough, and most of the time it might be, but what happens when you cycle into the shadow of a building, a tree-lined street or if you have cycled along my blind-side and into the shadow of my HGV? Those colours will no longer be as bright as you think they are. What if the Driver's eyes have been used to looking at sun-covered roads and suddenly they enter a building's shadow. Their eyes will need a bit of time to adjust and your 'bright' top or bag may not look so bright to them.

You need to stand out in this environment. I am looking for you but I am looking for you in a sea of quite dull colours. This becomes even harder in the two dimensional world of a HGV mirror. In the average 0.7 seconds I look into one mirror, and if the colours you are wearing are the same as your surroundings, then it is going to be more difficult for me to see you *quickly*…and I want to see you as quickly as possible because I have other areas I need to check.

Shine

I am going to start with 'Shine' as I hope that what I will show you is how Shine can help in all of the other 'S's'. This section is not going to discuss a shiny, sweaty face or metal bike frame catching the sunlight. I am going to relate Shine to being brightly coloured. 'Shining' is something that I would like to see more Cyclists think about while riding their bicycles. This is where I want to discuss High Visibility (Hi-Vis) clothing and Lights. I completely understand this is a contentious issue amongst Cyclists and some very prominent, highly respected UK Cyclists say that they shouldn't have to look like Health and Safety adverts to be able to jump on a bicycle. Cycling should be easy for everyone without making them feel like they need lots of equipment to do it. I agree with that. It is great to see public access bikes all over major towns and cities today. You should be able to jump on a bike in whatever clothing you are wearing, and ride to the station or work, or a meeting, or for a coffee with friends etc. The issue today though, is not everywhere has the infrastructure of separated cycle lanes; some people still feel put off by a perception of danger…and it has to be said, unfortunately driving culture and behaviour by some in this country has not yet fully accepted the Cyclist as an equal on the road: speed, training, licensing, myths about road 'tax', and insurance often being the arguments chucked at Cyclists. I want people to be able to ride a bicycle and feel safe but at the moment if you chose to ride a bicycle on the roads then you will interact with HGVs at some point, and this is why I would like you to at least read what is below regarding Hi-Vis and Lights with an open mind.

I know that studies have been carried out on the wearing of Hi-Vis clothing and some say that it does not help road users see Cyclists. I know that Cyclists have been involved and killed in collisions with cars and HGVs while wearing Hi-Vis clothing. This has led some to believe that makes Hi-Vis useless. I also understand that there are studies to show that Cyclists wearing Hi-Vis cycling clothing are actually seen as more 'professional' or 'experienced' by other road-users so it almost justifies worse behaviour when passing near to Cyclists as 'they can handle it' or 'are used to it'. I am sure these studies have foundation within the variables and criteria the researchers set but what I would like to add is that when I am sat in my *HGV*, with the height advantage that it gives me, a Cyclist in a Hi-Vis top is so much easier to see *more quickly* than someone in standard office wear or a coat....or even Lycra cycling gear.

Now I am not going to pretend I carried out a doctoral-level research piece but none of the studies that I could find were related to how Hi-Vis is seen by *HGV* Drivers, just car drivers. I do not know if research has been carried out regarding the visibility of Hi-Vis in relation to HGV Drivers but that is why I am going to discuss it below because I know that it can help at certain times. Whether you choose to accept my point is up to you but I'd like to discuss it.

I have had discussions with so many HGV Driving colleagues who say that Hi-Vis just helps them to see Cyclists when on the road. I know this is easily said but due to the height of a HGV Driver's seating positon Hi-Vis does help me see Cyclists more quickly. Hi-Vis gets Cyclists on my 'radar'. In faster moving traffic I am able to see a Cyclist 20, 50, 100, 200 meters in front of me. When in slow or stationary traffic, I can see 20, 50, 100, 200 meters behind me in my mirrors and see a Cyclist moving towards me so much easier than one in standard clothing. I am not saying I will not see you if you don't wear Hi-Vis clothing because I may but, in the 0.7 seconds I have to look in one mirror, I want to see you as quickly as possible.

Also, I am not going to pretend that just because you wear Hi-Vis clothing I am suddenly going to be able to see you in my Blind-spots. Of course I'm not. They are Blind-spots. As I have already discussed they are either Physical obstructions of the HGV design or the Observational Limitations caused by where the HGV Driver isn't looking. *BUT* Hi-Vis for me is not about seeing you when you are *CLOSE* to me, Hi-Vis is about seeing you *BEFORE* you get close me. I want to see you as quickly as I can and Hi-Vis can help me see you before you get so close as you enter a Blind-spot. I choose to wear Hi-Vis when I cycle as I know it can make a difference. You wouldn't think it sometimes when being overtaken by some drivers but I do choose to wear Hi-Vis when I ride my bicycle. Ultimately though, this is your choice.

Reflective Clothing

Now obviously Hi-vis clothing does not work at night and I completely grasp that it is going to be a pain to have to carry Hi-vis clothing and then reflective clothing if you happen to ride at different times of the day: it could be daylight on your morning commute and dark when you come home. Some cycling clothing does incorporate both but this tends to be small flecks of reflective material on a Hi-vis top. It is also worth remembering that reflective clothing only works when it is reflecting light. That may sound a bit obvious but on some reflective tops it only seems to 'reflect' when *my* headlights are on you and the light is being reflected back to the source. If you are to the side of me then those reflective strips don't actually work. As I say that is how *some* work but not all. I guess it depends on what type you have but how do you find out...?

I also understand that some people may not want to ride in cycling gear as you may be riding your bicycle to go out and don't want to have a Hi-vis top on when you walk into a bar. There are manufacturers making some great, 'normal looking' clothing now and these include jeans and coats that contain reflective thread within the item so it doesn't look like cycling gear. It does look amazing and definitely does the job but again this may not be everyone's' choice. Reflective clothing is great at night but poor during the day so, again, it comes down to your choice really.

Lights

Having discussed Hi-Vis/Reflective clothing above, I truly believe that it is your choice. When I am sat in my HGV, in my opinion, it can help me see you but I also understand that there are reservations as to whether it works. When it comes to lights though I want you to have them...I know I said this book isn't about telling you what to do but I may even go as far as saying 'please get them!'

In the UK if you are riding a bicycle at night it is the law that you fit them but I want you to have them during the day too. I do find it strange that motorcycles, by law and to help others see them, must have their lights on at all times yet bicycles, that are a lot smaller in width, do not need anything on during the day.

Day or night, lights are great at catching the eye of a HGV Driver. In fact, disregard that. *Flashing* lights are great at catching the eye of a HGV Driver. This is where I want you to think about your surroundings again and how you might blend in. Imagine I am looking into my HGV mirror. It is dull, overcast or at night. It is rainy and you have a non-flashing, fixed white light. Think about what type of light cycling bulbs tend to be: bright, LED, bluey light.

What colour are vehicle headlights nowadays? Bright, LED/XENON, bluey light!? Your 'fixed' cycling light blends into its surroundings. I can say hand on heart that your front light does become lost when my mirror is filled with car headlights. Can you spot the Cyclist in the right-hand image above?

Can you see them?

Pixilation aside, you can just make out the Cyclist above. A flashing light will not blend into the car headlights like a fixed light may. It also works in relation to rear lights too. If I am moving in traffic and I look forwards I am looking into a sea of rear red lights. Occasionally these will also become brighter because drivers will be applying their brakes. So I will see brighter, flashing red lights, and even fixed bright lights as a lot of drivers tend to keep their foot on the brake pedal rather than use their handbrake. Your rear light has to compete with the surrounding red light so keep that in mind when choosing a set of lights (these tiny, one L.E.D lights aren't any good).

I once spoke to a cycling campaigner who said she had discussed Cyclists flashing lights with a HGV Driver. She told me the HGV Driver had said it made it difficult for him to see how many Cyclists there were so he didn't like them, but I pointed out that it had obviously grabbed the Driver's attention and therefore he was now looking that little bit harder. Whether he liked them was not important. They had done their job.

Flashing lights will help a HGV Driver see you even more quickly compared to non-flashing lights at night but even during the day they are great at grabbing a Driver's attention. The human eye reacts to movement and the flashing light replicates movement but it is also brighter than the other movement surrounding the HGV Driver. In dull, overcast or rainy conditions a flashing light will make you stand out. In sunny conditions you have bright sections of road followed by dark shadows that are cast by buildings, trees or high vehicles and the flashing light will always enable other road-users to see you as their eyes re-adjust to the new light conditions. Flashing lights can be seen in the peripheral vision and I am always reacting to them.

They are certainly easier than carrying around a Hi-Vis jacket and if you can carry around a smart phone then you can carry a set of cycling lights.

If you don't have them then please consider buying some.

So with all of that in mind I want continue with the 5 S's.

Shape/Silhouette

The human brain and eye are naturally drawn to the head and shoulders of another human. It is difficult to get this across if you have never really had to look for a human shape, especially if you are surrounded by people most of the day. You just don't realise you are doing it. You will naturally look at peoples' heads as you recognise the head/shoulders shape of a human as this is how we interact. We know that the 'head' is where and how we communicate to one another. Now think about the type of bicycle you ride. If you ride a Dutch-style bike, that has you sitting more upright, you are more recognisable as a human shape. If you ride a road bike you are "a*se up, head down" as I once heard it described to me, and the natural head/shoulder silhouette is lost.

You become a smaller, rounder object that isn't instantly as recognisable...which is one dis-advantage you have when as other road users look for or react on seeing you.

I am not suggesting everyone go out and buy a Dutch/shopper-style bicycle but, as the Netherlands are often used as an example of 'cycling utopia', I would like you to consider the shape of the bicycle the Dutch use. These bikes are not built for speed but are built for comfort, and I would say a slower type of safer, cycling. I completely understand that they may be heavy so that is why they are slower but because they are slower that in itself could be seen as a reason that you will be safer.

You also have the added advantage that your seated position is more upright. This will mean you natural eye-line will be similar to when you are walking and will mean an increased ability to see. You may not want to ride a Dutch-style bike but think about the riding position of Bike Share bicycles across our Cities today and even the fold-up bikes available today. They are far more conducive to road safety and from my point of view, the riding position means HGV Drivers will instantly and intuitively recognise the natural head and shoulders shape of another human (certainly when compared to a racing road bike…personally, they just shouldn't be used on the roads for a commute in a busy urban environment).

Another reason to think about the more up-right style of bicycle is, reportedly, there have been less recorded incidents related to Bike share riders versus others Cyclists. This may be due to other road users thinking the Cyclist is less experienced, therefore giving more time and space (which is a positive for their use) but it cannot be denied that the riding position is more advantageous for visibility. If you choose to wear Hi-Vis too there will also actually be more surface area visible…just my thoughts.

One other area related to your Shape is your correct use of gears. If you have stopped at a junction and you are in too high-a-gear then it will be harder for you to pull away. I see this all the time. The legs need to pump harder so the body comes forwards off the seat, more weight is on the handle bars, the head goes down, the head and shoulders shape disappears, the bike starts to sway from side-to-side with each pump of the leg but most importantly, the natural eye-line of the Cyclist is then only looking a few meters in front of them, rather than at the road. This may not be the safest position for visibility when in a junction with a HGV.

Shadow

As I have discussed above, shadow is something that doesn't exist all the time but when it does exist you become harder to see.

The most obvious shadows to talk about are when it is sunny and the brightness of the sun causes buildings, trees, vehicles etc to cast shadows across sections of road. You and others could be using the road in bright, sunny conditions where your white or blue or red t-shirt will stand out but the moment you enter the shadow of the a HGV or a tall building those colours will no longer stand out.

That could just be the moment that the HGV Driver's eyes are also adjusting to the shadow or they are taking off their sun glasses to allow their eyes to re-adjust to the darker conditions. I know that may sound a bit sensationalist but it's not beyond reality. In fact it has happened to me. I was in stationary traffic and I wanted to take a picture to high-light just how contrasting shadow and brightness can be from a HGV Cab.

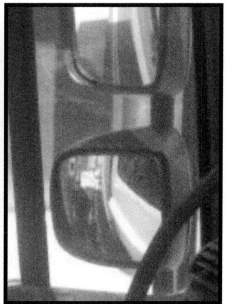

The picture I took actually captured a Cyclist that I hadn't seen. A flashing light would have made all the difference in this situation as the brown t-shirt did not stand out within the shadow of my HGV (also a good example of how the views differ in each Mirror).

Sound

Sound is quite important with regard to cycling as really, you don't make any. You have no engine that can be heard over other traffic such as motorcyclists or mopeds, therefore HGV Drivers will not hear you. Your positioning, your speed, brighter clothing (maybe), or fitting a flashing light (preferably) will help me and other HGV Drivers see you because your silent approach will never mean we hear you.

Summary

In the introduction I said that one day, I really hope this book doesn't matter and what I meant by that is that one day I hope this country sees the benefits of building local, regional and maybe even national *segregated* cycle paths that mirror some of our road infrastructure today. That would alleviate the need for others to 'see' you but at the moment that is not the case. Some towns and cities are embracing segregated cycle paths but they do not form any constant, flowing, continuous segregated cycling 'highways' and I think it will be a long time before significant segregated cycle paths are on all our roads. As a result you will interact with HGVs or large vehicles at some point if you use a bicycle. That is why I believe this chapter about 'Being Seen' is important. Being seen is still significant at the moment because the majority of our road infrastructure places Cyclists on the road with heavier, faster, metal vehicles and being seen may help you on that one occasion which now becomes a near miss rather than a collision...maybe??

Being seen is obviously the most important factor in helping you stay safe when interacting with HGVs. Key to being seen though is your positioning in relation to the HGV Driver's mirrors. You must allow the HGV Driver *time* to see you though. Speed may be good when trying to beat your previous race/distance time, or when trying to increase your average mile-per-hour, but trying to beat your previous commute, in rush hour, is not a good idea and is not the time for speed. This may mean you slowing down when near HGVs. This may even mean going out and organising a bit of training with a qualified Cycling Instructor. Obviously that is up to you. One thing you can certainly do is just remember that the safest place to be, with a HGV, in a junction is at the rear and to the side of that HGV.

I have tried to get across my thoughts on Hi-vis/Reflective clothing and wanted to try to get you to think about why they may help. I am not going to pretend that they will help all the time because they won't, but they are good at getting you on the radar of a HGV Driver *before* you get close to that Blind-spot. You can choose to wear it but I *am* going to say get hold of some decent flashing lights. Honestly, they are great. I promise.

Conclusion

There it is. Information and advice that I hope you have found interesting. I also hope that you'll find it useful and something you can use on the road. I wrote this because I wanted to try and help others stay safer. I cannot comment on other incidents between Bicycle and HGV as I was not there but the incident I saw was the result of a HGV Driver missing a Cyclist because of either failing to look properly, the limitations placed upon them, the attention-absorbing nature of the road or a combination of all, and a Cyclist unknowingly putting themselves in a place they should never have been. I want you to know what all of those potential dangers might be to help you stay safer.

I have shown you:

- How many mirrors HGVs have…but how that in itself leads to the creation of Blind-spots.
- What can be seen within each mirror, and more importantly what cannot…and why.
- The two types of Blind-spot: Observational limitations and Physical Obstruction.
- The variables that increase Observational Limitation Blind-spots.
- What the Physical Blind-spots are: Mirrors, Cab and Trailer.
- The left side of the HGV is called the 'Blind-side' even by trained, experienced HGV Drivers.
- The attention-absorbing nature of the road.
- The fluid nature of the road.

- How you can be missed when the HGV Driver simply turns their head.
- Why a HGV Driver will position their vehicle in a certain way: Defensive Driving and the Required Space.
- The concept of the 'Illusion of Space', and how it disappears.
- The contrasting perceptions of Filtering versus Undertaking.
- What happens when a HGV makes a Left or Right turn, and where the HGV Driver:
  - May look
  - Will look
  - Will not look
- What can happen in various junctions.
- How Left-hand drive HGVs will differ from Right-hand drive.
- How you blend into your surroundings.
- Hi-Vis can help but not all the time so it is up to you.
- Flashing lights definitely help but, again, it is up to you.

As a result I hope I have shown you that you cannot know where the HGV Driver is looking, so never assume you have been seen. There will still be collisions between HGV and Bicycle. It can be due to the behaviour of the HGV Driver and it can be due to the behaviour of the Cyclist. I am not naive enough to think that all HGV Drivers are perfect or that all Cyclists will know what is happening within that HGV Cab, but I just don't want *you* to put yourself in unnecessary danger based purely on you not knowing what the danger is.

You may be thinking 'Why is it down to me?' And I understand your thoughts. After all you are a 'Vulnerable road user' and you should be looked out for, but what I hope I have shown is that sometimes you may be missed, either due to your size, your speed, the road layout, the 'attention-absorbing' nature of the surroundings, the manoeuvre being carried out, the Blind-spots, where the HGV Driver has to look or feels they must look, the fluid nature of the road or just a result of Filtering versus Undertaking…and, I accept, the unprofessional behaviour by *some* HGV Drivers (not all but some).

There is one comment that is often used and (to paraphrase) that is how 'HGVS account for only 5-6% of traffic but are responsible for 50% of Cyclist road deaths'. That originally came from a particular year and was based on London statistics but it has become a comment used by some as a general understanding of the dangers of HGVs. I am not going to argue with the numbers as I am sure there is a truth to it but if HGVs are only 5-6% of traffic in the urban area, so the chances of seeing one are small, then please treat then differently if it is your decision to do so. They are not cars. HGVs do not allow the HGV Driver to see as well as a car driver…as I have shown you throughout this book. Ultimately, it is about working together. It is about understanding one another's limitations and concerns. HGV Drivers will be car drivers, they may be Motor-Cyclists and they may be Cyclists (I know several) but if they are not Cyclists then there is a very good chance, in the UK at least, they will have done a day's training as a Cyclist (search for Driver CPC 'Safe Urban Driving' course). HGV Drivers do need other road-users to understand that this need to look around their vehicle does take time. The need to look in certain places means you may not be where the HGV Driver is looking. It may only be a few seconds but it could be those few seconds that causes an incident between you and a HGV.

As I have mentioned in the introduction, this book is about decreasing *your* chances of becoming involved in an incident with a HGV. I know this is a small number and I know this book is not a silver bullet to Bicycle/HGV incidents. Everyday there are hundreds of thousands of miles travelled by HGVs across the UK, and without incident. The majority of HGV Drivers are professional and I know from experience that I probably stopped at least half a dozen collisions a day (when in London) because I was pre-empting other road-users' behaviour (so if I am doing it then others are too). There are HGV Drivers doing the best they can to make sure they are never involved in any type of collision on our roads but, there are those that may not be. You may interact with a HGV Driver who is at the beginning of their shift and are nice and refreshed from a few days off, or you might interact with a HGV Driver who is at the end of a 6 day week and at the end of a 14 hour day (just because it is your Monday morning, does not mean it is their Monday morning). You may interact with a HGV Driver who was seconds before endangered by a dangerous driver and they are still calming down so forget to look in a certain mirror. You may interact with one who doesn't know the area (you may use the same route everyday but by the very nature of logistics the HGV Driver may never have been there before). They may be following Sat-Nav directions, or a printed map, or even their smartphone map location beacon. They may be an agency/stand-in relief driver so may never have done that route before or driven that make of HGV Before. They may never have actually taken a British driving lesson, let alone a test and are learning the culture of our roads (that wasn't a political point but it is a reality of HGV Driving and UK roads today). Or, you may be interacting with the greatest, safest HGV Driver in the world but they happen to be looking left into their 3 mirrors, when you happen to be on their right. Those are just some of the realities of being on our roads.

When you cycle I want you to remember the statement I used earlier. It really is a rhetorical question because you now know the answer.

Have I Been Seen?

And the only answer you can have is

I Can't Know

As your answer is 'I can't know' then I hope that helps you in your decision-making.

Writing this book may be a way of dealing with what I saw that day but I hope some good has come from it. I am sorry it has taken me so long to write and get it into the hands of those that could benefit from it. I just hope that some have not been injured, or killed, that may have been prevented by having read this book. I know the chances are small but that is one thought that has kept me going…

I really hope this book helps you on the road. I am sure this book will generate criticism from those that are not open-minded enough to accept that this might help in some small way, but if you have read just one little section and have said to yourself 'I didn't think of that', or 'that's actually a good point' then I have been successful.

Ultimately, if this book makes you feel a little more informed and feel safer then I have done what I wanted to do. Thank you for taking the time to read this book, I really appreciate it. You are now HGV AWARE.

Stay Safe,

Richard

Printed in Great
Britain
by Amazon

31309428R00129